Praise for *Becoming Better*

"We spend so much time trying to do more, but true success comes when we learn to be better. In *Becoming Better*, Ryan Gottfredson, PhD, provides a practical and inspiring guide for anyone looking to elevate their thinking, unlock their capabilities, and create a more fulfilling life."

JON GORDON, bestselling author of *The Energy Bus* and *The One Truth*

"The key to Our Working Together Leadership and Management System to create value and growth for all the stakeholders and the greater good starts with who we are. In *Becoming Better*, Ryan Gottfredson, PhD, provides a powerful, science-backed guide to personal development, helping individuals to dramatically improve their 'being,' which will enable them to serve the greater good with love and humility."

ALAN MULALLY, former CEO of Boeing Commercial Airplanes and former CEO of Ford Motor Company

BECOMING
BETTER

BECOMING BETTER

The Groundbreaking Science of Personal Transformation

RYAN GOTTFREDSON PhD

Cataloguing in publication information is available
from Library and Archives Canada.
ISBN 978-1-77458-582-5 (paperback)
ISBN 978-1-77458-584-9 (ebook)

Page Two
pagetwo.com

Cover, interior design by Jennifer Lum
Interior illustrations by Jeff Winocur

ryangottfredson.com

Also by Ryan Gottfredson

Success Mindsets: Your Keys to Unlocking
Greater Success in Your Life, Work, & Leadership

The Elevated Leader: Level Up Your
Leadership Through Vertical Development

Contents

Introduction

*Life is a process of becoming, a combination of states
we have to go through. Where people fail is that they wish to
elect a state and remain in it. This is a kind of death.*

ANAIS NIN

YOU AND I HAVE SOMETHING IN COMMON. We both want to become even better than we are now.

But our motives for becoming even better may differ. And that is okay.

Why do you want to become better?

Do any of the following statements resonate with you?

- I possess an inherent desire to grow and improve myself.
- I want to be a better person for the people I love.
- I want greater fulfillment and happiness.
- I want better and more fulfilling relationships.
- I want life to come more easily to me.
- I want greater professional or monetary success.
- I want to be more respected or achieve greater social recognition.
- I want greater health and well-being.
- I want to contribute more positively to society.
- I have spiritual or moral beliefs that compel me to become better.
- I have to get better or I may face the consequences of losing out on something or someone.

Regardless of your motive for picking up this book, I am glad you did. This book is going to change how you think about becoming better, and it is going to dramatically improve your ability to become better. Here is why: This book is not about changing your behaviors, or simply doing better. It is about improving and elevating your *being*.

How I Came to Write This Book

Ever since I can remember, I have had a deep desire to become better, which I think originally came from a place of insecurity. When I was growing up, my parents always met my physical needs, but they were rarely there for me emotionally. So as a child and teenager, I longed for love, connection, and attention, and I felt that if I could only become better, I would get the emotional fulfillment that my body craved.

As a teenager, one way I sought out love, connection, and attention was through trying to become better at basketball. If I could only become the best basketball player, I would be more liked, more connected, and more respected.

This line of thinking is probably why I found myself in a sports psychology class during my senior year of high school. I was excited to take the class because I believed it would help me get better at basketball, which in turn would fill my emotional needs.

While I am not sure the class helped me become much better at basketball, it did change the trajectory of my life because it gave me an insatiable desire to continue learning how to become better. This class was my first exposure to reading self-help and leadership books, and I was captivated by the books I read by the famous basketball coaches Pat Riley, Mike Krzyzewski, and Rick Majerus. I remember thinking to myself, "If I could write books like these someday, I would have the best job."

But I had no clue how I could make the study of becoming better my career until I met a Harvard Business School professor when I was 20. Intrigued by his position, I asked him what subject he taught. He told me, "Organizational behavior." Not knowing what that subject was, he went on to explain it to me. I remember the thought that popped in my head: "This sounds like sports psychology, but for business." From that conversation, I knew I had found a career path focused on becoming better.

Wanting to establish a foundational understanding of how people become better, I took a meaningful step down my desired career path when I entered a doctoral program in organizational behavior at Indiana University. The focus of my dissertation was on leadership, which allowed me to review the prior 70 years of leadership research. One of my biggest observations from this review was that the vast majority of leadership research was focused on one question: "What do leaders need to *do* to be effective?" That is a good question, and it has led to some very helpful answers. But to me, the question felt shortsighted because I believed (and still do) that leadership is not just about *doing* certain things; I believed that leadership is about *being* a certain type of person, someone that others want to follow.

Upon graduation from Indiana University, I became a management professor at California State University, Fullerton, where I have spent the last 11 years diving deeply into how leaders and people become better. Recognizing that what I was learning from my research could help business leaders become better, I established my consulting business. My business now allows me the frequent opportunity to work deeply with organizational leaders to help them elevate in their leadership and their impact. Leveraging my learnings and my consulting experience, I have written two previous books, *Success Mindsets* and *The Elevated Leader*, both of which connect to core aspects of the process of *becoming better*. And, throughout this time and these efforts, I have continually been trying to apply my learnings to myself so that I can keep becoming better.

The Big Problem

Through my extensive efforts learning and researching about how to become better, personally trying to become better, and helping other people become better, I have discovered a big problem. The problem is that most people do not actually have clarity on how to *become better*.

I have learned that there are two dominant personal development paths we can take: One path focuses on *doing better*, and the other focuses on *being better*.

The *doing better* path is what is most focused on, most known, and most travelled. Think about our educational systems, athletic programs, and almost all organizational and leadership development programs. They spend nearly 100 percent of their focus on helping people gain knowledge or develop skills that will help them *do* better. While this path can be helpful, such development rarely translates into transformationally becoming better.

Exposing the Limitations of the *Doing Better* Developmental Path

To demonstrate the limitations of the *doing better* developmental path, let me give you an example: a former coaching client of mine, Sheryl.

I began coaching Sheryl because her boss had told me that he saw potential in her but felt stuck in his efforts to help her realize that potential. So he asked me if I could help. To set up the connection, Sheryl's boss initially introduced us via email, and Sheryl responded with excitement to start our coaching process.

At the bottom of her email signature, I found it interesting to see that Sheryl had multiple strings of letters after her name, along with several stamps representing professional certificates. I remember thinking to myself, "Why does she need coaching? She's clearly engaged in a lot of developmental efforts."

When we met for an introductory call, I asked her how she felt coaching could help her in addition to the various degrees and certifications she had received. I must have struck a sore spot because she quickly expressed her frustrations about feeling perpetually stuck as an individual contributor in her organization and being passed over for promotion, year after year after year.

She then told me that after every year of missing out on promotion, she would go get either a new degree or new training certificate to make her "more qualified" for a leadership position. By this point, she was feeling like she was overqualified for her position and stunted in her career. I felt heartbroken hearing that she was losing hope in a brighter future for herself and her career.

Her development up to this point was focused on the only approach she knew: the *doing better* development path. She was unaware that there is a better, more transformational way: the *being better* path.

This became clearer to me the more I got to know Sheryl. I discovered that what was holding her back was not a lack of knowledge, skills, or experience. It was a lack of self-confidence. While she was someone who did a great job when she was given a task to complete, she was fearful, anxious, and timid when opportunities arose for her to take initiative. She consistently second-guessed herself.

The reality is that if she wanted to get unstuck and get promoted, she needed to hop on the *being better* development path: She needed to transform and heal her relationship with herself, rise above her insecurities, and become willing to step into fear, uncertainty, and even problems and failures. Until she could do those things, she would continue to stay stuck.

This book is not about
changing your behaviors,
or simply doing better.
It is about improving and
elevating your *being*.

_____

Why the *Doing Better* Developmental Path Has Not Worked for Me

As I reflect on my own development journey, I have seen this same phenomenon. Like most people, I have struggled and failed a lot. And looking back, my approach to overcoming my struggles and failures was to focus on *doing* better rather than *being* better. Let me give you some examples.

When I was in high school, my biggest goal was to get a college scholarship to play basketball. That scholarship never came. While I had spent a lot of time on the *doing better* development path, consistently practicing to become a skilled player, I now look back and see that the primary reason I didn't get a college scholarship was because I was not a very good team player. I was more focused on my personal performance than my team's. As a result, we struggled to win games, leading to few college recruiters being interested in our team or any of us players. I had less of a *doing* problem and more of a *being* problem.

When I was in my doctoral program, I failed my first comprehensive exams. It wasn't that I wasn't smart enough to pass them, it was because I was more focused on publishing research papers and getting accolades from my professors and peers than on learning and mastering the basic concepts of organizational behavior. Again, I had less of a *doing* problem and more of a *being* problem. In hindsight, I feel fortunate to have failed because it forced me to do work on my *being*, which not only helped me pass my comprehensive exams the next year, but also changed how I have approached learning, growth, and mastery ever since. In a way, my failure helped me step on the *being better* development path without even realizing it at the time.

Two years into my job as a professor at California State University, Fullerton, I took a leave of absence to do some consulting work for Gallup. After about 10 months in that job, I got fired. It wasn't because I didn't have the knowledge or ability to do my job; I got fired because I had self-protecting mindsets that were holding me back from being a valuable contributor to my division. Again, what was less of an issue was my knowledge, skills, and abilities, and what was more of an issue was my *being*'s ability to get the most out of my capabilities.

Each of these experiences left me extremely frustrated. I had the skills necessary to be successful, and I felt like I was doing the right things. But clearly, how I was operating was falling far short of my potential.

What about you? Have you ever felt like you were following "best practice advice" for personal development but felt frustrated that you fell short of your desires? My guess is that you have felt these, or similar, frustrations. That is the natural byproduct of focusing on the *doing better* development path.

The Solution

You'd think that I would have learned my lesson sooner, but it took getting fired from Gallup for me to wonder if there was a different developmental path that I needed to consider. It turns out there was: the *being better* path.

As I have come to learn more about it, what I have discovered is that the *being better* development path is not well-known. In fact, from my experience introducing it to people, less than 1 percent have even a vague understanding of this path and what it is all about.

In this context, I feel incredibly fortunate to have found the *being better* path. It has allowed me to do the deep inner work of focusing on my *being*, not on my *doings*. And the difference has been transformational.

By walking down the *being better* developmental path, I feel I have grown and developed exponentially. To give you a sense of this, I started putting concerted effort toward this strategy about eight years ago. After about four years, I remember thinking to myself, "I have grown more in the last four years than in the prior 14 years of my adult life." And now, four years later, I feel I have grown more in the last four years than in the prior 18.

In fact, it was only after I started focusing on elevating my *being* that I developed the courage to take big strides toward my goals, which included starting my own consulting business, writing books, and developing an online community designed to help people become better. As a result, I have been fortunate to observe this *being better* developmental path having a transformational impact on thousands of others that I have worked with. And I want you to experience this transformation too.

The Purpose of This Book

I have written this book to help you become better in whatever way you desire. I want you to take massive steps toward becoming more of the person you want to become. I want you to get to a place in the not-too-distant future where you can look back on who you were and feel like you are living life at a higher, more fulfilling, and more impactful level than you had previously. I want you to feel like you have transformationally become better.

For this to happen, you will need to take three steps, which correspond to the three parts of this book.

- The first step is to better understand what your *being* is. The more we understand our *being*, the better we can do at improving it. This will be the focus of part 1.

- The second step is to deepen your self-awareness and awaken to the current quality of your *being*. The more we awaken to our *being*, along with identifying and understanding higher levels of *being*, the greater the clarity we will have about the process of *becoming better*. This will be the focus of part 2.

- The third step is to learn about the practices you will need to engage in to actually transform and elevate your *being*. This will be the focus of part 3.

Now, as we are about to get started on these three steps, I imagine that what I have proposed—improving and elevating your *being* and transformationally *becoming better*—may sound like a lot, and even a little scary. You may even wonder if pursuing this route will cause you to be a different person or lose your identity. And you probably wonder how long it will take and if it is worth the effort. These anxieties are normal.

Let me assure you, you will continue to be the same person. What we are aiming for is an upgraded and more sophisticated version of yourself. It is my goal to walk you through these steps in an easy and digestible manner. I don't want you to feel overwhelmed. I want you to feel hopeful about who you can become and what life can be like when you are a more elevated you.

Now, I can't do the work for you. You'll have to do that on your own. But I will be giving you directions and resources that will make this feel manageable. I will be rooting for you from a distance. And I will give you some ways in which I can continually support you along the way.

Regarding the length of this path, I have some good news and some bad news. Bad news first: there is no end to this path. The reality is that we can always become better no matter how good we are. But the good news is that once you get started on this path, you will initially feel your rate of growth dramatically increase. And, based on my experience, as you continue on that path your rate of growth and transformation will only speed up. There just won't ever be a finish line.

If that is okay, let's start this journey and begin laying the foundation for living life on a more elevated plane, becoming more of the person you desire to be, and having more of the impact you desire to have. Let's work toward *becoming better*.

Chapter Features

After having some beta readers read this book, they requested that I add on two short sections at the end of every chapter.

The first thing they asked for was a summary of key discoveries that one should have made as a result of reading the chapter.

The second was applications for leadership. The beta readers were aware that I have written this book for anyone who wants to become better. But my primary audience in the work I do is business leaders. So they requested a short summary of applications for leaders specifically. If you're a leader, these segments will be an additional nudge for how you can further elevate yourself to elevate your impact!

Key Discoveries

- There are two developmental paths: a *doing better* path and a *being better* path.

- *Doing better* is the path most taken, but it is generally only incrementally helpful, at best.

- *Being better* is the path least taken, but it is the only path that will lead to us transformationally *becoming better*.

- The three keys to taking the *being better* developmental path are: coming to a greater understanding of our *being*, awakening to the current quality of our *being*, and engaging in efforts to upgrade and improve our *being*.

Applications for Leadership

How focused are you on becoming better? In my work with leaders, I have discovered that the majority are much more focused on *doing* better than *being* better. Most leaders want to know the three or five things that they need to *do* better so that they can check the box for having done them. They care more about accomplishment than they do about transformation and *becoming*, which is a strategy that can be beneficial in the short term. But what I have learned is that the leaders who focus more on *being* better than *doing* better are not only the most effective leaders but have an increasingly positive impact over the long term. So, consider: What is your developmental strategy? Are you more focused on improving your *doings* or your *being*?

PART 1

To Become Better, You Must Become Familiar with Your Being Side

1

We Have a Doing Side and a Being Side

Becoming is not a contradiction of being but the epiphany of being.
ANANDA COOMARASWAMY

I F YOU WANT to transformationally become better, one of the most important ideas to learn and connect with is this: You have two different sides of yourself, a Doing Side and a Being Side.

Your Doing Side is the one you are quite familiar with. You have probably focused on it a lot in your development efforts.

Your Being Side is likely to be less familiar to you, and you probably have not focused on it much in your development efforts. Yet it is this side that you need to focus on if you want to transformationally become better.

To bring these two sides of yourself to life, let me use a well-known sports coach as an example: Bobby Knight.

Bobby Knight is one of the most well-known and controversial basketball coaches to ever pace a sideline. He is most known for his tenure as the head basketball coach at Indiana University, my alma mater, from 1971 to 2000, during which time he guided the Indiana Hoosiers to three NCAA National Championships. He was inducted into the Naismith Memorial Basketball Hall of Fame in 1991.

Knight passed away during the fall of 2023. In the wake of his death, sports commentators gave their perspective on his legacy. Across my reading and listening to these commentaries, one word seemed to be repeated over and over again: "conflicted."

People are conflicted about Knight because, on the one hand, he is respected as having one of the best basketball minds. He was an ingenious tactician and strategist. Jay Bilas, a lead college basketball analyst at ESPN, called him a "brilliant, brilliant coach and bigger than life." But on the other hand, he was notorious for his anger issues and reviled for his sometimes extreme behavior. There are highlight reels filled with him flinging a chair across the court during a game, headbutting a player, choking a player, grabbing a player's jersey and jerking him to his seat, kicking at a player, shoving fans, cursing out the Big Ten commissioner from midcourt, kicking a megaphone, and banging on the scorer's table during a game.

While being a brilliant coach, he struggled to regulate and lead himself. And he is not alone. There are many public figures that seem to be immensely talented but have operated in a manner that leads the public to question their character. Some examples are Bill Clinton, Lindsay Lohan, Shia LaBeouf, Naomi Campbell, Michael Jackson, Tiger Woods, O.J. Simpson, Gordon Ramsay, Elizabeth Holmes, Carly Fiorina, Kenneth Lay, and Elon Musk.

These are all well-known figures who, based on how they have operated, seem to be greatly developed on their Doing Sides, but not very developed on their Being Sides.

The Two Sides of Ourselves

Our Doing Side

Our Doing Side represents our talents, knowledge, skills, and abilities. It is our capability to *do* certain things. A simple way to think about our Doing Side is: How many tools do I have in my tool belt, and what is the quality of these tools? People with more and higher-quality tools can do more than people with fewer and lower-quality tools.

When it comes to Bobby Knight, he was very developed along his Doing Side. Bilas wrote, "In my view, he could have coached any sport and coached it just as effectively as he coached basketball. He had an analytical mind, understood motivation and inspiration, and had an extraordinary ability to break things down." Bilas is suggesting that, amongst coaches, Knight stood out as one of the most talented, knowledgeable, skillful, and able.

A quick way for you to gauge how developed you are along your Doing Side is to consider what knowledge, skills, and abilities you possess that allow you to do things better than others or do more things than others. For example, if you went to medical school, you would have gained the knowledge and skills needed to perform medical procedures that most people are not able to perform. Possessing such abilities would indicate that you are more highly developed along your Doing Side than most people.

We generally have a decent sense of our Doing Side. We largely know what tools are on our tool belt and how high-quality those tools are. And when we focus on improving along our Doing Side, we are on the *doing better* developmental path discussed in the Introduction.

Our Being Side

Interestingly and unfortunately, we are generally not as in touch with the second side of ourselves: our Being Side.

Because we are not as familiar with it, and because it is more complex, how to fully understand and connect to your Being Side will take some explanation over the next several chapters. So, for now, I will simply define our Being Side as our ability to regulate and lead ourselves. A simple way to think about our Being Side is that it is not related to the number or quality of tools in our tool belt. Our Being Side is about the quality and sophistication of the person wearing the tool belt. Perhaps the most common way people refer to our Being Side is by calling it the quality of our personal character.

Coming back to Bobby Knight, while Jay Bilas sang praises about Knight's Doing Side, it was his Being Side that Bilas felt conflicted about. Bilas wrote:

> I had the privilege of knowing Knight well, and calling him a friend. We worked together at ESPN, and would go on annual golf trips during the summer. He was the only friendship I ever had that I felt I had to explain or justify. After all, while Knight's positive traits were numerous, so, too, were his questionable ones. He was capable of incredible acts of kindness and thoughtfulness, yet also capable of questionable acts of stubbornness and thoughtlessness.

One way for you to gauge how developed you are along your Being Side is to consider how well you can stay emotionally regulated in situations of stress, pressure, uncertainty, and discomfort. I'll give you more and deeper ways to gauge the quality of your Being Side as we go along.

When we focus on developing along our Being Side, we are engaging in the *being better* developmental path discussed in the Introduction.

Bringing the Two Sides of Ourselves Together in One Framework

Our Doing and Being Sides are both important and serve us in different ways, so we need to consider how developed we are along each side of ourselves.

To help you with this, I have created a two-by-two matrix, with low and high Doing Side on the horizontal axis and low and high Being Side on the vertical axis, that can be used to identify where you're operating from.

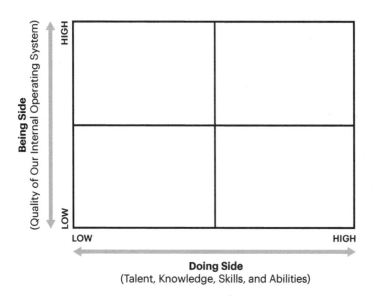

I want you to deeply connect to this framework because as you do, you'll start to gain greater clarity about yourself and, in particular, your Being Side. To facilitate this, I am going to address four questions that naturally arise when people are presented with this framework:

1   What quadrant would we ideally like to operate from?
2   Where do most people operate from?
3   Of the two sides, why do most development efforts focus on the Doing Side?
4   Which side holds people back from becoming their best selves?

1. What quadrant would we ideally like to operate from?

Of course, the quadrant that is most ideal to operate from is the high Doing and high Being quadrant. Those who operate here are the most impactful and successful people. These are the types of people we look up to and aspire to be. And if we happen to fall within their circle of influence, they have a positive and uplifting impact on our lives.

Notable people who seem or have seemed to operate in the high/ high quadrant include:

- Abraham Lincoln
- Susan B. Anthony
- Mahatma Gandhi
- Martin Luther King, Jr.
- Nelson Mandela
- Jacinda Ardern
- Brené Brown
- Satya Nadella

For each of these people, do you feel like their ability to be a positive influence on the world was more because of their Doing Side or their Being Side? My sense is that the power of their influence comes much more from their Being Side, and I believe you will understand why that is as you learn more about the Being Side.

Unfortunately, the high Doing/high Being quadrant is where the fewest people operate from.

2. Where do most people operate from?

Most people operate from the low Doing and low Being quadrant. To understand why that is, let's take this one side at a time, starting with our Doing Side.

Research on star performers conducted by my dissertation advisor, Herman Aguinis, has found that across academics, scientists, athletes, entertainers, and politicians, performance does not follow a normal distribution. What this means is that across a field of performers, we do not find that most hang around a moderate level of performance, with few performing at high or low levels. Instead, performance generally follows a power-law, or Pareto, distribution. This means that most performers are not average but operate at a low level, with only a small number at a high level, more than what would be predicted by a normal distribution. See the image below for a depiction of these two types of distributions. The darker shade shows the typical power-law distribution of performance in a given field as compared to the standard bell curve, which represents a normal distribution.

Normal Distribution Overlaying a Power Law Distribution

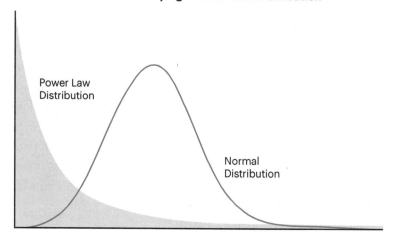

To bring this performance distribution to life, consider the field of music. Most people do not even know how to play an instrument or sing beyond a basic level. Thus, most people fall near the far left-hand side of their Doing Side for music knowledge and skills. Slightly to the right of these people are individuals who possess a bit of experience playing an instrument or singing. For example, my son has been learning how to play the drums for the last two years. He knows the basics, and while he is not very refined, he is further along his Doing Side than most people, though still far from the high end.

But as we zoom out and consider the entire spectrum from novices to the most talented musicians, we find that professional musicians, those high on their Doing Side, make up a very small percentage of the population. And we find more people at the far right end of the Doing Side than what would be predicted with a normal distribution. For example, Beyoncé has 32 Grammys, Sir Georg Solti has 31, Quincy Jones has 28, and Alison Krauss and Chick Corea both have 27. In fact, there are 18 people or bands who have won over 20 Grammy Awards. These are all outliers on their Doing Side, and make up the far right tail of the power-law distribution.

Now, I just used the field of music as an initial example, but research on star performers has found that this same distribution seems to exist in any field of expertise, such as tennis, medicine, or leadership. This suggests that while some people might be at the high end of their Doing Side for a particular field, most people are near the low end for most skills and abilities. The simple reality is that most people do not have exceptional talent, knowledge, skills, and abilities.

For example, when it comes to playing basketball, I suspect that I am better than 90 percent of the population, but my talent is well below that of professional basketball players. Perhaps this puts me right on the line between low and high on my Doing Side.

Now, let's move to the Being Side.

Here a similar distribution exists, with most people operating from a position of low Being. To bring this to life, we need to step into the field of developmental psychology.

The primary emphasis in developmental psychology has historically been on investigating how children mature. What has been found is that as children go from infants to adults, they go through a number of developmental stages that represent different levels of maturity and cognitive and emotional sophistication. This makes sense when we compare an 18-year-old to a 2-year-old. Eighteen-year-olds have greater abilities to regulate their cognitions and emotions than 2-year-olds. This regulatory ability is not related to an individual's Doing Side knowledge, skills, or abilities, but rather to their Being Side.

Interestingly, because developmental psychology has historically focused on child development, very little emphasis has been placed on adult development. A big reason for this is that for a long time, essentially from the 1880s to the 1960s, developmental psychologists assumed that people stopped developing when they became adults.

It wasn't until the 1960s that a select few developmental psychologists started to study adult development. And they have made some fascinating findings over the last 60 years.

One finding is that adults can also develop in their cognitive and emotional maturity.

Just as with childhood development, there are adult development stages that represent different levels of cognitive and emotional maturity. In fact there are three primary adult development stages, which are representative of our elevation along our Being Side. So, people at the base adult development stage possess less cognitive and emotional maturity and operate with a lower level of Being than people at the higher stages. We will be covering these stages in depth later in the book.

In children's development, almost all kids naturally develop as they get older. But researchers have found that developing as an adult does not come naturally. In fact, they find that most people do not develop along their Being Side in adulthood. Specifically, developmental psychologists report that 64 percent of adults operate at the first stage of adult development, a low level of Being; 35 percent operate at a moderate level; and only 1 percent operate at a high level.

The fact that few people ever elevate along their Being Side is summarized well by one of my favorite authors, Andy Andrews, who is most known for his book *The Traveler's Gift*. He has written:

> Most people, like the mockingbird, will sing the same song as an adult that they sang in their youth. In other words, left alone, most people tend not to change very much. Most people are threatened by new information. Why? Because new information requires us to remap our minds, and sometimes that includes changing what we believe.

If we mapped the adult-development percentages to a distribution curve, what we would find is a power-law distribution curve, just like what we find along the Doing Side. Thus, connecting the research on star performers with that on adult development, findings suggest that most people operate from the low Doing/low Being quadrant.

Now, if someone operates from the low Doing/low Being quadrant, does that make them a bad person? Of course not. I do not think that most people are bad. But I do believe that most people are stalled in their development and are not living up to their potential for the person they can be and the positive impact they can have within their spheres of influence.

3. Of the two sides, why do most focus on developing the Doing Side?

The vast majority of our development efforts focus on our Doing Side, what I referred to as the *doing better* developmental path in the

Introduction. In his book *Hidden Potential, New York Times* best-selling author and Wharton Business School professor Adam Grant states, "When we say success and happiness are our most important goals in life, I'm curious about why character isn't on the list. What if we all invested as much time in our character skills as we do our career skills? Imagine what America would look like if the Declaration of Independence granted every citizen the right to life, liberty, and the pursuit of character."

Consider our education system. How much does it focus on the Doing Side as opposed to the Being Side? Almost all education efforts and curriculum focus on gaining knowledge and skills. There is rarely any concerted effort geared to improving students' character, self-regulation, and self-leadership. Consider college classes. When I take an accounting class, I expect to learn how to do accounting tasks. I don't expect that class to improve my ability to effectively navigate the stress, pressure, uncertainty, and complexity of daily life. Our education system is primarily focused on helping us add tools onto our tool belt. It is not very focused on upgrading the person wearing the tool belt.

The same goes for our athletic programs. Most athletic programs emphasize the gaining of skills that can be employed during competition. We focus on helping baseball pitchers throw harder and use different types of pitches. We focus on helping basketball players add new moves to their repertoire or improve their ability to use their off hand. And we focus on helping soccer players better control the ball. We are great at helping a lot of people develop elite-level skills. But not all people with elite-level skills perform at an elite level. What generally separates the very best from the really good is not their skills, but their Being Side. The very best have greater self-confidence, are more resilient, and can handle pressure much more effectively. Yet very few athletic development programs focus on helping players develop their self-confidence, resilience, and stress tolerance.

Once again, the primary focus of athletic development is on adding tools to the tool belt, not on upgrading the person wearing the belt.

In organizations, development efforts are rarely any different. Employee and leadership development generally starts with a needs assessment, which identifies knowledge or skill gaps. With those gaps identified, programs are developed to close them. For example, it is not uncommon for a needs assessment to identify emotional intelligence as a skill gap. With this gap identified, organizations send employees and leaders to workshops focused on improving their skills associated with emotional intelligence. In these workshops, the employees and leaders are given the best tips on what to *do* to operate with greater emotional intelligence. But it is one thing to know what emotionally intelligent people *do* and *how* they operate. It is a completely different thing to have the self-regulatory abilities to actually *be* emotionally intelligent. Again, the primary focus of organizational development is on adding tools to one's tool belt, not on upgrading the person wearing the belt.

Frances Hesselbein, the former chief executive of the Girl Scouts and leadership thought leader, has said it this way: "Leadership is a matter of 'how to be,' not 'how to do.' You and I spend most of our lives learning 'how to do' and teaching other people 'how to do.' Yet, in the end, we know it is the quality and character of the leader that determines the performance and results."

Because of the emphasis on the Doing Side in leadership development, we know that most leaders are near the high end on that side. Further, developmental psychologists who have studied the adult development stages of business leaders have found that 85 percent of all leaders operate in the second stage. Seven percent of leaders operate in the first stage, and only 8 percent of leaders operate in the third stage. This means that most leaders operate in the high Doing/low Being quadrant of the 2x2 framework. They have developed knowledge, skills, and abilities (i.e., the tools) to allow them to succeed as individual contributors, which in turn has made them prime candidates to be promoted into leadership positions. But just because someone is successful as an individual contributor does not necessarily mean they have the Being Side capacity to lead a team or organization effectively.

Finally, take into consideration personal and leadership development books and how people choose to ingest them. Many of these books are like Stephen R. Covey's *The 7 Habits of Highly Effective People*. They are great and insightful guides, but they are focused on identifying the three, five, or seven things that people need to know or *do* to operate effectively. There are other books that, in my opinion, focus more on our Being Side and seek to help people become better. Some of these books are *Dare to Lead* by Brené Brown, *The Infinite Game* by Simon Sinek, and *Think Again* by Adam Grant. These books invite us to investigate the quality of our Being Side and our normal patterns of processing and operation. But commonly, when I talk to people who read these types of books, their critique is that there isn't a lot of clarity about what they need to *do* differently. They were hoping for the simple three or five steps or a tool to add to their tool belt, rather than being prompted to take a deep look at themselves.

The reality is that the vast majority of developmental efforts and programming focuses on improving our Doing Side and overlooks our Being Side. This is unfortunate for at least three reasons:

- First, most of us are not taught how to take a deep look at ourselves and investigate the quality and sophistication of our Being Side.

- Second, most of us fail to recognize that while having more and higher-quality tools is beneficial in life, what is most important is the maturity, quality, and sophistication of the person wearing the tool belt. It is one thing to have great tools, but if you can't employ those tools effectively, they are of little benefit.

Something I have come to learn is that the more people elevate along their Being Side, the more they get out of their Doing Side.

- Third, the key to truly and transformationally becoming better is by focusing on developing along our Being Side.

4. Which side holds people back from becoming their best selves?

Let's start answering this question by looking through two opposing lenses: (1) what do people commonly struggle with and (2) what characteristics make people great.

A quick Google search of the things people most commonly struggle with included these results:

- stress
- anxiety
- depression
- self-doubt
- addiction
- relationships
- finances
- life changes

Reviewing this list, do you think that most people struggle with these things because of deficiencies on their Doing Side or deficiencies on their Being Side?

While Doing Side deficiencies surely play a role in these common struggles, the primary reason people find themselves struggling to rise above these challenges is related to our Being Side. Let's dive into each of these struggles, and their common roots.

Anxiety, Depression, Self-Doubt, Addiction, and Life Changes

When people struggle with anxiety, depression, self-doubt, addiction, and life changes, it is generally not because they are lacking on their Doing Side and do not possess certain knowledge, skills, and abilities. Further, people aren't going to work their way out of these issues through Doing Side development of their knowledge and skills. You don't alleviate anxiety and depression by gaining knowledge about anxiety and depression.

But if you learn about why these issues exist, you will quickly discover that they are generally rooted in brain network dysfunctions that impair one's regulatory abilities, which is directly connected to our Being Side. If people want to rise above these issues, they will need to adjust and improve their brain's functionality, which is a necessary part of improving along our Being Side.

Relationship Issues

When people struggle with relationships, it is generally because they have Being Side deficiencies that cause them to operate in a manner that prevents healthy connection. Let me give you two quick examples focusing on attachment styles and attention deficit hyperactivity disorder, or ADHD.

First, psychologists have found that people possess one of four attachment styles: secure, avoidant, anxious, or disorganized. People with secure attachment styles generally have healthy relationships. People with the other three styles may know things they should do in a healthy relationship and even have the ability to do those things, but their Being Side holds them back from practicing healthy relationship behaviors. For example, someone with an avoidant attachment style may know the value of being vulnerable in a relationship and may have the skills to express vulnerability, but when their partner reaches out for emotional connection, their Being Side directs them to distance themselves from their partner. This is because people with an avoidant style tend to feel uncomfortable with close connection. Our attachment styles are connected to our Being Side, not our Doing Side.

Second, researchers have found that people with ADHD commonly struggle with communication and organization, both of which can significantly impact the quality of a relationship. ADHD is not related to Doing Side deficiencies of knowledge, skills, or abilities. It is related to the self-regulatory abilities of one's Being Side.

These are just two of many examples that I could draw upon to suggest that most relationship issues are much more rooted in one's Being Side than Doing Side.

Money Issues

What about money issues? Do people struggle with their finances more because they lack knowledge about money and how to deal with it, or more because they struggle with impulse control or considering the future?

Personally, while I have never had significant money issues, for most of my adult life I have not been happy about my money situation. This wasn't because I didn't have knowledge and skills related to money. Quite the opposite! My bachelor's degree is in finance. But what I have come to learn is that for most of my life, I had a deficit mindset as it relates to money. I felt that the best way to grow wealth was by playing safe and saving as much of a fixed pie as possible. This mentality included me having a lot of fear around losing or misinvesting my money.

After working on my relationship with money, which is more connected to my Being Side than my Doing Side, I have developed more of an abundance mindset. I am no longer preoccupied with the fear of losing or misinvesting my money, nor am I focused on capturing as much of a fixed pie as possible. Instead, I am focused on being more strategic and growing the size of the pie.

By making this shift in my Being Side and improving my cognitive and emotional maturity as it relates to money, I experienced two significant benefits. First, I was able to upgrade the person wearing the tool belt, which made me more capable of employing the financial tools I developed when obtaining my finance degree. Second, I enhanced my capacity to move past my fears and toward my dreams. Originally, I did not want to be an entrepreneur because I was afraid of putting my family's financial well-being at risk. But with my new mindset, while I still recognized the risk that comes with entrepreneurship, I began to see it as a way to increase the size of my pie. With this new outlook, I became willing to step into my fears and take on debt to establish my business. While this was scary at the time, it was a decision that opened a world of opportunity for me in almost all facets of my life. I would not be writing this book now had I not engaged in this Being Side development.

Across These Common Issues

I hope you recognize a theme across these common issues: When people are struggling with navigating life, it generally has much more to do with their Being Side than their Doing Side.

The vast majority of my consulting work involves working with business leaders, and I believe this theme holds true across the board with the leaders I work with. If leaders are struggling or simply not operating up to their potential, it is generally not because they lack knowledge and skills. Typically they are in the position they are in because they already possess the required knowledge and skills. The primary reason I see leaders struggle is because they lack the requisite level of cognitive and emotional maturity, which often causes them to step left when they should step right.

What Characteristics Make People Great

Next, let's consider characteristics that make great people great. A short list of these characteristics includes courage, humility, patience, empathy, integrity, resilience, generosity, and adaptability.

Think about these characteristics. Do you think people like Susan B. Anthony, Mahatma Gandhi, and Nelson Mandela obtained them or fulfilled their personal aspirations through a focus on improving their Doing Side knowledge, skills, and abilities? Or do you think these examples of greatness developed the characteristics by refining their Being Side mindsets, psyche, and regulatory abilities?

I don't know about you, but I feel like I know about courage, humility, patience, empathy, and generosity, and I even know how to employ those qualities. But despite my knowledge and skills associated with them, there are times when my Being Side prevents me from being courageous, humble, patient, empathetic, and generous. Stated differently, I believe that the struggles I have with these characteristics have much more to do with my Being Side than my Doing Side.

Let's now come back to Question #4: Of the two sides—Doing Side or Being Side—which one holds us back from becoming our ideal selves? The answer seems pretty clear. If we are hung up in any facet of our lives, it generally has more to do with our Being Side than our Doing Side. Yet our Being Side gets relatively little attention.

In my own life, I have come to realize that the struggles I have had with self-confidence, my relationships, and my finances have much more to do with deficiencies in my Being Side than my Doing Side.

What about you? Take a moment to consider the struggles you have had in your life, and for each, ask yourself: Was this struggle more because of a deficiency in my Doing Side or Being Side? I believe that if you are honest with yourself, you will find that your struggles have been most strongly rooted in your Being Side.

If we are hung up in any facet of our lives, it generally has more to do with our Being Side than our Doing Side.

———————————

Key Discoveries

Coming to an understanding that we have a Being Side in addition to our Doing Side has been a game-changer for me and for those I work with in leadership and personal development. This is because coming to understand and connect with our Being Side opens up the *being better* development path, which is like knowing the secret key to unlocking the best version of ourselves.

Here is the reality:

- Very few people know they have a Being Side or are in touch with it.

- If we are falling short in some way in life, it is generally more because of a deficiency in our Being Side than our Doing Side.

- Since almost all development work across our educational settings, athletic programs, and organizational development systems focuses solely on our Doing Side, our primary and typical approach to improving ourselves is to do likewise.

- Yet, personal transformation always involves an upgrade and elevation in our Being Side.

- If very few people know they have a Being Side, even fewer people know how to improve and elevate along it.

- Thus, if we can connect with our Being Side and learn how to improve and elevate along it, we will possess the key to unlocking personal transformation, a key that many people want, but few know exists.

While these discoveries are great, we have only just begun connecting with and understanding what our Being Side is. Are you ready for more?

Applications for Leadership

As a leadership development consultant, I help leaders learn about, awaken to, and improve along their Being Side. Through this work, I have seen those I have coached become more emotionally in-control and regulated in the following ways:

- They have developed the capacity to let go of limiting beliefs that have held them back from greatness,

- They have risen above fears of uncertainty to take bold and impactful action, and

- They have become less "me"-focused and more "we"-focused.

These shifts have been transformational.
Now consider:

- Have you recently experienced any of these transformational shifts?

- How much of your development efforts are focused on your Being Side relative to your Doing Side?

2

What Is Your Being Side?

Without the ability to end things, people stay stuck,
never becoming who they are meant to be, never accomplishing
all that their talents and abilities should afford them.

HENRY CLOUD

ONE OF MY SON'S favorite movies is *The Wild Robot*, an adaptation of a book under the same title written by Peter Brown. In this movie, which is set in the future, a company called Universal Dynamics produces dynamic robots that are programmed to accomplish any helpful task given to them.

At the beginning of the movie, a cargo ship is caught in a typhoon, causing six robots to be lost at sea and eventually washed ashore on a remote island uninhabited by humans. On shore, one of these robots gets accidentally activated by an animal. This robot is nicknamed "Roz," and she is the main character in the movie.

Having been programmed to accomplish any helpful task, Roz ineffectively interacts with a variety of wildlife, seeking to be assigned a helpful task to accomplish. After repeatedly failing to connect with the animals Roz encounters, the robot hunkers down in an observation and learning mode for several days in order to learn the animals' language.

After learning the animals' language, she again tries to seek an assignment to be helpful. In the process, she gets chased by a bear. As she runs away from the bear, she stumbles down a hill, accidentally smashing into a goose nest, killing the mother goose and crushing all but one egg. Shortly thereafter, the egg hatches, and the baby gosling imprints itself onto Roz. With the help of a friendly possum, Roz realizes that she now has an assigned task: to raise the gosling to be able to eat, swim, and fly by fall.

Being of advanced technology, Roz is able to recognize that she has not been programmed to raise a baby goose and thus needs to adopt new programming to be successful at accomplishing her task. The rest of the story shows Roz continually misstepping in small ways because of the limitations of her embedded programming and then adapting her programming to meet the demands of her task. In the end, she develops a very emotional, loving relationship with the goose, something she was not originally programmed to do.

(If you want more of the story, I recommend watching the movie. But fair warning, your eyes might start leaking.)

Unlike Roz, we didn't start off life preprogrammed. But during our upbringing, our minds and bodies became programmed to survive our childhood. For some of us, that might mean being programmed to seek great accomplishments in order to receive the love and affection of our caregivers. And for others it might mean being programmed to stay quietly hidden, not causing any problems, or be a people pleaser to avoid being punished by their caregivers.

But make no mistake: Like Roz, your mind and body have been programmed to interpret your world, think, and operate in specific ways. And, also like Roz, we might do well to ask ourselves: Is my programming set up to most effectively navigate my life, its various demands, and my future?

The answer to this question is likely "not fully." I want to explain why that is, and in doing so, we'll deepen your understanding of what your Being Side is and the significant role it plays in your life.

What Is Our Being Side?

Roz, like all computers, had an internal operating system. Roz's operating system controlled and regulated her, operated automatically, undergirded everything she did, and contained programming that she was prone to replicate. For example, she was initially programmed to give a sticker to every animal she encountered, which she dutifully did, even though it was annoying to these animals and worked against her being accepted by them.

Carrying this analogy forward, what do you think: Do you have an internal operating system? Do you have a system within you that controls and regulates you, operates automatically (even subconsciously), undergirds everything you do, and contains programming that you are prone to replicate? And do you have any programming, like Roz, that leads you to do things that actually work against your goals?

The answer to these questions is "yes." You do have an internal operating system. Under the control of your nervous system, your operating system is responsible for effectively regulating your body's internal world of emotions and feelings as you interact with your external world. It not only operates automatically and often subconsciously, but it also directs almost everything you do. Psychologists have reported that at least 90 percent of our thinking, feeling, judging, and acting are driven by our internal operating system's subconscious automatic processing. And it sometimes holds you back, gets in your way, or limits you.

To help you get a sense of your internal operating system and how it impacts how you operate, I invite you to explore some of your internal programming. Do you have any *if-then* programming, where *if* something happens, *then* you automatically and subconsciously respond in a certain way? For example, consider the following questions:

- *If* you receive constructive criticism, *then* are you prone to get defensive?

- *If* someone cuts you off while driving, *then* are you prone to get angry?

- *If* you are feeling vulnerable, *then* do you move away or armor up to protect yourself?

- *If* your organization initiates a significant change, *then* are you prone to resist it?

- *If* your child doesn't respond to one of your requests in a timely fashion, *then* are you prone to lose your patience?

It is important to recognize two things about these examples.

First, the *then* aspects are generally automatic, knee-jerk reactions that help you to regulate uncomfortable emotions. And while these reactions may help you feel more comfortable, they may not be the most optimal.

Second, our internal operating system has the ability to override our Doing Side knowledge and skills. Here is the reality: We may know about patience and even have the skills to be patient, but our body may not possess the programming to actually *be* patient when we get cut off while driving or our children don't promptly respond to us. Therefore we should recognize that the automatic, nonconscious reactions of our operating system are not connected to our Doing Side, but rather our Being Side.

This leads us to a deeper definition of the Being Side: It is the quality of your body's internal operating system. We'll expand this definition in the next chapter, but for the rest of this one, I want to ensure that you fully grasp that you do indeed have an internal operating system. Let's explore how it functions.

How Our Internal Operating System Functions

We all have a bodily system that is responsible for the functioning of our internal operating system and the overall quality of our Being Side.

This system is our nervous system.

The nervous system is our body's command center. It is the major controlling, regulatory, and communication system in the body. It is a complex and highly organized network that is designed to direct us away from pain and toward pleasure, however we might define pain and pleasure.

While our nervous system performs a number of different jobs to achieve this, including homeostasis, reflexes, and balance, in the rest of the chapter I will go into detail about how our nervous system controls and regulates our Being Side's internal operating system. While the ideas I will be presenting are a bit technical, they will help you gain clarity on what your Being Side is and what you will need to do to upgrade it in order to *become better*, which we'll get into in part 3.

There are six functions involved in how our internal operating system works that are important to understand. Let me walk you through each.

Function 1: Our Internal Operating System is Always "On"
The first function of your internal operating system that you need to understand is that it is always running. It is always

- attuned to our survival
- on alert for any indications that our safety is in question
- sending messages from our senses to our brain to inform it of our current status.

Function 2: Our Internal Operating System Directs Us Away from Pain

The second function of our internal operating system, and its most primary job, is to help ensure that we respond to our environment in a manner that directs us toward pleasure and away from pain. Ultimately, our internal operating system is wired and attuned to helping us stay alive as well as stay on track to fulfill our needs, whatever those might be.

Function 3: Our Internal Operating System Uses a Four-Step Process

The third function of our internal operating system is to serve as the constant communicator between our body's senses and our brain so that we can process and navigate our environment in a manner that is aligned with how we define pleasure and pain. This communication between body and brain occurs through a near-simultaneous, four-step process:

The Four-Step Process of Our Internal Operating System

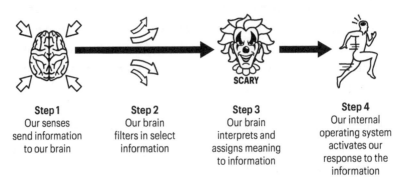

Step 1	Step 2	Step 3	Step 4
Our senses send information to our brain	Our brain filters in select information	Our brain interprets and assigns meaning to information	Our internal operating system activates our response to the information

Step One: Our internal operating system *uses our senses* to continually take in information from our environment and then sends this information to the door of our brain. But not all this information is going to make it through the door and into our brain.

Step Two: At the door of our brain, our internal operating system filters out irrelevant information and only filters in what it deems as important information for our fulfillment of pleasure and avoidance of pain.

A key aspect to understand about Step Two is that our brain is limited in its processing abilities. It cannot process all of the information brought to it by our senses.

Let me give you a quick example of this. All day, your body has been sending signals from your toes to your brain. But, if you are anything like me, you really haven't noticed your toes. However, now that I have brought your toes to your awareness, it is likely that your brain has now filtered those senses in, so you are currently conscious of your toes.

Understanding the doorway to our brain also clarifies why two different people might encounter the same situation, but one person picks up on a feature of it that the other person misses. For example, when my wife, Jena, was little, her brothers had her watch the horror movie *It*, and she has been fearful of clowns ever since. For me, clowns don't pose any sort of threat. So, on Halloween, when we go trick-or-treating with our children, it is not uncommon for her to say, "Did you see that scary-looking clown costume? That freaked me out!" And for me to respond by saying, "I didn't, I guess I wasn't paying attention." The reality is that I probably glanced at the clown costume, but my nervous system did not filter it into my awareness because, to my internal operating system, it was not a threat.

Step Three: Our internal operating system then processes and interprets the information that has been filtered in through the door.

When signals get filtered into our brain, our internal operating system then automatically assigns meaning to those signals. We call this "meaning-making."

Our internal operating system assigns meaning to these signals in a manner that is most likely to keep us safe and protected in the moment, and this meaning-making is heavily influenced by our past experiences. For example, when my wife and I see a clown, we react in different ways that are shaped by our past experiences. Jena's internal operating system immediately and automatically interprets clowns as a threat. My operating system takes more time to assign meaning to a clown in terms of whether it is scary or funny. Either way, our internal operating system is doing its job of assigning meaning to the information it takes in.

Step Four: Our internal operating system determines the appropriate response that our body should make based on the information filtered in and how it has been interpreted.

Step Four is where the rubber meets the road in this four-step process. Once signals get to our brain, filtered in, and then interpreted, our internal operating system activates our response to that information. It is this automatic and generally nonconscious response to stimuli that directs the majority of our behavior and operation.

Continuing with the clown example, when my wife sees a clown and interprets it as a threat, her internal operating system will automatically send adrenaline throughout her body, causing her to get tense, her palms to sweat, and her heart to race. In this state, Jena struggles to stay calm and balanced and is prone to do things that might seem unreasonable, like scream unnecessarily. This is her internal operating system making adjustments to help ensure her safety. For me, when I see a clown and I don't interpret it as a threat, I am not on edge and can navigate that situation in a more calm, balanced, and reasonable manner.

The final three functions that we need to know about our internal operating system build off of this four-step process.

Function 4: Our Internal Operating System Processes Automatically and Nonconsciously

The fourth function of our internal operating system is that this four-step process generally occurs automatically and nonconsciously. By automatically, I mean that we do not have to do anything to activate the four-step process and we cannot stop it from occurring. By nonconsciously, I mean that our internal operating system engages in this process below our conscious awareness.

Function 5: Our Internal Operating System Develops Patterns of Processing

The fifth function of our internal operating system is that it develops patterns of interpretation (Step Three) and response (Step Four) to the common signals that it takes in.

The purposes of these patterns are to enhance speed of processing and conserve energy. If we are in danger, the faster our body can take in, interpret, and respond to information from our external world, the better our body can adapt to protect us. Also, when our internal operating system goes through the four-step process, it consumes energy. And the longer it takes to go through the process, the more energy it consumes. So, if our internal operating system can engage in the four-step process efficiently, our body can invest its energy in other functions.

As mentioned previously, one way to identify some of your patterns of processing is by creating *if-then* statements related to your programming. Let me give you several examples that I have seen and consider whether you have similar patterns of interpretation and response.

- *If* my wife sees a clown (stimulus), *then* she will see that clown as being dangerous (interpretation) and will move to protect herself or get defensive (response).

- *If* Ian is cut off while driving (stimulus), *then* he feels disrespected (interpretation) and reacts in a way to make the other driver aware of their disrespect (response).

- *If* Tori receives constructive criticism (stimulus), *then* she takes the criticism as an attack (interpretation) and gets defensive (response).

- *If* a stranger smiles at Tom (stimulus), *then* he feels uncomfortable (interpretation) and avoids eye contact (response).

- *If* Cory receives a compliment (stimulus), *then* he feels like the spotlight is on him (interpretation) and he downplays the compliment (response).

- *If* a colleague asks Melissa to help (stimulus), *then* she feels that if she says "no" she will be rejected by that colleague (interpretation), so she says "yes" to any requests for help (response).

We all have thousands of patterns of interpretation and response built into our internal operating systems that have been developed over time and across the situations we have encountered. And let's be real: Some of these programming patterns are more productive and helpful than others.

Function 6: Our Internal Operating System's Patterns Can Be Changed

The final function of our internal operating system might be the most important for us to understand: Our operating system's patterns of interpretation and response can be changed, refined, and upgraded.

To *become better* you
will need to upgrade your
nervous system such that
you adopt more mature and
sophisticated patterns of
interpretation and response.

———————————————

In fact, to *become better* you will need to upgrade your nervous system such that you adopt more mature and sophisticated patterns of interpretation and response.

To bring this to life, I want to introduce you to one of my heroes from afar: Brené Brown. I do not personally know her, but I feel like I do because of her raw authenticity in the books she has written.

Brené Brown is a professor and social worker who has become a near household name because of her books, TED Talks, podcast, and programming on Netflix and HBO Max. Six of her books have been number-one *New York Times* bestsellers: *The Gifts of Imperfection, Daring Greatly, Rising Strong, Braving the Wilderness, Dare to Lead*, and *Atlas of the Heart*.

In each of her books, she shares examples of how she has awakened to patterns of processing that originally felt right and good to her, but were ultimately limiting. And she discusses how, upon learning about these patterns, she has disrupted and upgraded those patterns to transformationally *become better*. I want to share two of these examples here.

Her book *The Gifts of Imperfection* is all about helping people live wholeheartedly, as opposed to living in a state of shame, fear, and disconnection. The content for this book comes from her research comparing people who live more wholeheartedly and those who don't. Across her exploratory research, she identified several themes among those who live wholeheartedly, one of which was stillness.

This finding was disruptive to her because, as she wrote, "I wish I could tell you how much I resisted even hearing people describe stillness as an integral part of their wholehearted journey... I am sure my resistance to this idea comes from the fact that just thinking about meditating makes me anxious."

She expounded on this idea to identify an aspect of her automatic *if-then* programming: *If* I am invited to be still, *then* I will have to create a quiet emotional clearing where the truth of my life might catch up to me (interpretation), which makes me feel anxious and resist (response).

Through surfacing this programming and recognizing how this was holding her back from living more wholeheartedly, she started to work on upgrading her programming with the help of her therapist. Through this effort, she began changing how she defined stillness. She started to realize that stillness is not just about "sitting cross-legged on the floor and focusing on that elusive nothingness." Instead, it is "about creating a clearing. It's opening up an emotionally clutter-free space and allowing ourselves to feel and think and dream and question."

By reprogramming her body's internal operating system from interpreting stillness as boring, anxiety-inducing, and something she was not good at, to interpreting it as creating a clearing in one's life to feel and live wholeheartedly, she was able create space for stillness practices. And as she engaged in these practices, she was able to live more wholeheartedly.

Next, in *Daring Greatly*, she explores a programming pattern that felt so right, but was simultaneously so limiting. This pattern is associated with vulnerability, and it is one that resonates with me because I have learned that I have a similar programming pattern.

To get into this example, you need to understand that *Daring Greatly* emphasizes three primary points:

- Courage is required for living a wholehearted life.
- Vulnerability is required for courage.
- The fear of vulnerability prevents us from possessing the courage required for wholehearted living.

With her usual authenticity, Brené Brown highlights her struggles with coming to terms with the value and importance of vulnerability. Reflecting on a conversation with her therapist, she stated: "I frickin' hate vulnerability... I can't stand opening myself to getting hurt or being disappointed. It's excruciating... I hate how it makes me feel... It makes me feel like I'm coming out of my skin."

So for most of her life, whenever feelings of vulnerability would arise, she would armor up and avoid stepping into those feelings. She wrote that she was wired to "keep everyone at a safe distance and always have an exit strategy."

This programmed aversion to vulnerability felt right and good to her because it helped her feel more emotionally settled and in control. But it came at a cost. It caused her to be controlling at times, regardless of how that made others feel. And it was limiting to her because it prevented her from being courageous and living wholeheartedly.

Daring Greatly is an inspiring journey focused on her experience of upgrading her internal operating system to become more willing to step into the discomfort of vulnerability so that she could be more courageous, loving, connecting, and value-creating. And she provides sage advice on how we can upgrade our own operating systems to do the same.

I hope that when you reflect on these two examples, you will recognize that it is possible for one to have the Doing Side knowledge of the value of stillness and vulnerability, and even possess the ability to be still and vulnerable. But in order for one to embody stillness and vulnerability, which are both key to living and operating at a higher level, it requires one to upgrade their Being Side programming.

Through these two examples, Brené Brown clearly articulates that she has installed an upgrade to her Being Side programming, allowing her to live life at a higher altitude. When she was at a lower Being Side altitude and was presented with the opportunity to be still or be vulnerable, her nervous system would get anxious and direct her to run. That was a reaction that felt right because it moved her away from her anxious and uncomfortable feelings. But what she failed to appreciate was how limiting this programming could be. It prevented her from being healthy, being courageous, and living wholeheartedly. But by elevating her Being Side altitude, she enhanced her regulatory control. Moving forward, when presented with the opportunity to be still and be vulnerable, she possessed the ability to slow her body down and be present with the temporary discomfort of stillness and vulnerability, which opened the door for her to respond to those situations in more value-creating ways. She was able to be healthier, bring a better version of herself to the situations she encountered, better connect with others, become more courageous, and live more wholeheartedly.

We all have programming that feels right but at the same time is holding us back. By exploring your programming, you will be given the opportunity to upgrade your Being and elevate your life like Brené did.

Key Discoveries

In chapter 1, you learned that you have a Being Side. From this chapter, you should now understand these ideas:

1   Your Being Side is effectively the quality and sophistication of your internal operating system.

2   Your internal operating system plays a foundational role in how you process, interpret, and respond to your world.

3   Your internal operating system has developed patterns of processing that largely operate automatically and below the level of your consciousness, dictating almost everything you do.

4 Because of your nervous system's desire to direct you away from pain and toward pleasure, it is likely that you have developed patterns of processing that are designed to protect you and help you feel safe and comfortable in the short term. But they may hold you back from being the person you want to be and having the impact you want to have.

5 To *become better* and become more of the person you want to be, you'll need to get in touch with the programming built into your internal operating system (you will do this in part 2) and investigate whether any of this programming needs to be upgraded (you will get direction for this in part 3).

I loved using Brené Brown as an example in this chapter because she is someone who has authentically demonstrated that it is possible to transformationally become better, and that the key to doing so involves upgrading the programming associated with our Being Side. She has given me hope that I can make similar transformational changes in my life to become more of the person I want to become. I hope she does the same for you.

Up next, we'll start to explore how and why some people possess higher-quality and more-sophisticated internal operating systems than others.

Applications for Leadership

Leaders are not immune from developing their own patterns of processing. And, of course, some leaders have developed higher-quality patterns of processing than other leaders.

Across my work, I have found that when leaders are misstepping in their leadership, these missteps aren't generally the result of a lack of knowledge or skills. Rather, they are almost always rooted in suboptimal patterns of processing. Let me give you a few examples.

- Some leaders shut down the ideas and suggestions of those they lead. This is generally the result of a pattern of processing where their internal operating system automatically and nonconsciously interprets others' ideas as a signal that they are losing control, not smart, or not respected.

- Some leaders avoid change. This is generally the result of a pattern of processing that interprets change as something that will lead to problems or prevent them from hitting their short-term milestones.

- Some leaders micromanage their employees. This is generally the result of a pattern of processing that informs them that if they don't do the work themselves, it won't get done right.

If such leaders are ever going to become great leaders, they are going to have to awaken to and reprogram their internal operating systems.

3

Individuals' Being Sides Differ in Altitude

An arrogant person considers himself perfect.
This is the chief harm of arrogance. It interferes with a
person's main task in life—becoming a better person.

LEO TOLSTOY

NOW THAT YOU KNOW that we have a Being Side, and that our Being Side is the quality of our internal operating system, I have a question for you.

I want you to imagine that we have 100 people in a room. Clearly, it would be rather easy to line them up based on their height, from shortest to tallest. But would it be possible to line them up based on the quality of their internal operating systems, from least- to most-sophisticated?

By now, you should sense that the answer to this question is "yes." Just as people vary in height, they vary in the quality and sophistication of their internal operating systems. Those with lower-quality operating systems function at a lower altitude along their Being Side than those with higher-quality systems.

But how could we distinguish the actual altitude of these individuals' Being Side? How can you distinguish the altitude of your own Being Side? I am going to give you actual measurement tools in part 2, but for now, let's conceptually work through it.

Expanded Definition of Our Being Side

To start, let's revisit and expand our definition of the Being Side. Previously, I defined it as the quality of our internal operating system.

Now, I want you to think about our Being Side as the degree to which our body's internal operating system is wired for value creation as opposed to self-protection.

Leveraging this definition, if we are lining the 100 people up from low Being Side to high Being Side, we would find those on the left to be more wired for self-protection, and those on the right to be more wired for value creation.

But what does that mean exactly?

The Wiring for Self-Protection

When someone's internal operating system is wired for self-protection, their body automatically and nonconsciously processes, interprets, and responds to the signals in their world in a manner that is designed to protect them from negative feelings and experiences in the moment. While our self-protective programming might feel right or justifiable, the consequences of such programming generally have three characteristics:

- First, self-protective programming usually only benefits us by helping us feel more safe and secure in the short term.

- Second, it is "me-focused," which means that we are directed to do what will make us feel good, which commonly causes us to operate in a way that is limiting or detrimental to others within our sphere of influence.

- Third, it limits us in the long term.

Let's go back to Brené Brown to bring this to life. Her original programming to avoid stillness and vulnerability helped her to avoid the uncomfortable feelings that came up for her when she was invited to be still or vulnerable. While that felt good to her, what she didn't fully appreciate was that her lack of stillness and vulnerability prevented her from living healthily and wholeheartedly.

As another example, my son once had an athletic coach that would say very mean and rude things to his players after they made a mistake, particularly his son. Why would a coach ever do this? Because he has self-protective programming. When his players mess up, his body has a hard time sitting with the discomfort of those mistakes, so he responds in a manner that helps his body feel better in the moment. But while this "me-focused" programming helps him feel better, it is limiting and detrimental to his players. And, ultimately, his players performed more poorly as the season went on because they increasingly played out of fear of being rudely reprimanded.

The Wiring for Value Creation

Conversely, when someone's internal operating system is wired for value creation, their body automatically and nonconsciously processes, interprets, and responds to the signals in their world in a way that creates value in the long term. This often means that their operating system has developed a tolerance for putting up with negative feelings in the short term so that they can create massive value for themselves and others into the future.

We saw this as a part of Brené Brown's transformation. To *become better*, she needed to upgrade her internal operating system so that rather than reacting to opportunities to be still and vulnerable in self-protective ways, she could respond to those opportunities in value-creating ways. She has now become someone who is willing to wade into the unsettling feelings associated with stillness and vulnerability because her body better recognizes that the long-term, value-creating rewards of being still and vulnerable far outweigh any temporary discomfort.

Check in with yourself for a moment. How willing are you to step into vulnerability? For me, this is an area where I need some Being Side development. And I suspect I am not alone. In fact, when I do 360-degree feedback surveys with executives that focus on the quality of their Being Side, I generally find that the aspect of their Being Side that they struggle with the most is their willingness to be vulnerable.

I know that if I can upgrade my internal operating system's programming to become more willing to step into the discomfort of vulnerability, I will be able to better connect with others, touch others' lives, and live wholeheartedly—all value-creating outcomes.

Four Key Insights About Our Internal Operating System's Programming

To dive deeper into this notion of being wired for self-protection versus value creation, I'd like to highlight four key insights about the programming of our internal operating system.

Insight 1: Our Internal Operating System Is a Meaning-Making System

The primary and best way to gauge our altitude along our Being Side is to investigate how our internal operating system is programmed to make meaning of our world.

As I mentioned in chapter 2, our body's internal operating system is responsible for picking up information from our senses, sending it to our brain, and, if it's deemed important enough for further processing, interpreting that information. When our operating system engages in this interpretation process of assigning meaning to the signals filtered in, what it is doing can be called "meaning-making."

Now, does everyone who sees or experiences the same signals interpret or "make meaning" of those signals in the same way? No.

A simple reality is that two different people can see or experience the same thing, yet their bodies' internal operating systems automatically and nonconsciously make meaning of the experience in different ways. For example, stillness can be seen as something that is scary and should be avoided, or as something that is a necessary part of living healthily and wholeheartedly. Vulnerability can be seen as a sign of weakness, but also as a sign of strength and as necessary for building trust and positive relationships.

So, to truly get a sense of how wired we are for self-protection versus value creation, we are going to have to investigate the quality of the ways we make meaning of our world and our situations. We'll dive deeply into this in part 2.

Insight 2: The Quality of Our Programming Exists on a Continuum

None of us are 100 percent wired for self-protection or value creation. So the second insight is this: The quality of our programming lies somewhere along the continuum between the two extremes.

A challenge for you is to try to determine where your programming is along this continuum.

Something that makes this difficult is that we surely possess value-creating programming around some things, but self-protective programming about others. For example, I can imagine that you make meaning of stillness as an essential part of living healthily and wholeheartedly, but that you are more self-protective when it comes to vulnerability.

In my work with leaders, I find that most fall somewhere near the self-protective end of the continuum with regards to failure. They see failure as something to be avoided and as an indication that they are a failure themselves. As a result, most leaders are slow to adopt new and less-proven strategies. While this makes them feel safe and secure in the short term, it ultimately limits the agility of the organization or team that they lead. But there are a few leaders who view failure in value-creating ways. They see it as an opportunity to learn, grow, and become a greater value creator in the future. Leaders who fall on the value-creating side of the continuum are much more effective at navigating the complexity of their environment than leaders who have a more self-protective relationship with failure.

It is only after we see the broad spectrum of how you make meaning of a variety of things that we can fully gauge the degree to which you are wired for self-protection or value creation. For now, consider the following:

- How do you make meaning of failure: something to avoid or something to approach?

- How do you make meaning of disagreement or conflict: things to avoid or things to approach?

- How do you make meaning of risk: something to avoid or something to approach?

- How do you make meaning of constructive criticism: something to avoid or something to approach?

- How do you make meaning of people performing below your expectations: people to avoid or people to approach?

When answering these questions, don't just think about how you make meaning of these things when you are in a context that feels safe and comfortable. Think about how you make meaning of them when you are feeling pressure to perform. I have learned that gauging your meaning-making leanings when there is pressure to perform is the best way to get an accurate reading of where your internal operating system falls on the continuum between self-protection and value creation.

Insight 3: The Programming of Our Internal Operating System Feels Right and Good

Whether we are programmed to make meaning in self-protective ways or value-creating ways, our programming feels right and justifiable. People who are wired to move away from stillness, constructive criticism, and vulnerability can defend their programming by talking about how each makes them feel bad or uncomfortable. And people who are wired to move *toward* stillness, constructive criticism, and vulnerability can point out the value they can create for themselves and others over the long term.

This insight, right here, reveals the biggest hurdle in my efforts to help people awaken to their Being Sides. In my work, I invite people to explore how they are programmed to make meaning of their world. And, as I have done here, I present various examples of self-protective and value-creating programming, and I invite people to reflect on their own programming.

Would it shock you if I told you that it is common for people to quickly get defensive and resistant when I invite this level of introspection? From my experience, this defensiveness and resistance is the result of people strongly identifying with their meaning-making patterns and feeling very justified in them. I mean, most of us have carried these patterns around for our entire lives, and we have done so for a reason. So, if we possess patterns of processing, it is likely that we believe they are ideal and are serving us in a valuable way. This was Brené Brown. If you read her books, you will see just how resistant she was to changing her programming associated with stillness and vulnerability, among other factors.

Let me share a notable example where I was doing a workshop and a high degree of defensiveness and resistance arose. This workshop involved a group of site supervisors from a construction company, and I was trying to help them see that the more they focus on avoiding problems, the more inclined they will be to micromanage. I suggested that rather than focus on avoiding problems, they should try to focus on a purpose that creates value, such as the construction of a beautiful facility. And I shared how I have found that when leaders are more focused on a value-creating purpose, it helps them to stay out of the weeds and lead from a more elevated level.

Upon saying this, I had a gentleman aggressively stand up and, just short of yelling, he said, "You do not get our business. If a problem happens on my site, I will lose my job!" He made a valid and justifiable point. Yet, it was a self-protective point. And it was also extremely revealing of two things: First, he was feeling a lot of fear and insecurity in his role; and second, he was operating as a control-oriented leader who was strongly prone to micromanage.

Now, if we possess self-protective programming, and we do, does that make us bad people? No, not usually. But it does surely limit how much value we can create.

I invite you to be open to the idea that while the way you make meaning of your world might feel right and justifiable to you, it may not be the best way to make meaning if you want to become a more positive influence on the world around you.

Insight 4: Our Window of Tolerance Reveals the Quality of Our Internal Operating System

You should be starting to realize that people who are more programmed for value creation have a wider window of tolerance for short-term discomfort than those who are more programmed for self-protection.

If you are not familiar with the "window of tolerance" concept, psychologists use the term to indicate the degree to which a person can remain regulated and function well in the face of stress, difficulty, or discomfort. But it has a deeper meaning when we connect back to our nervous system.

Our autonomic nervous system is the aspect of our nervous system responsible for regulating the body's physiological processes in response to our environments. It performs this regulatory process via two subsystems: the sympathetic and parasympathetic nervous systems. The sympathetic system is commonly referred to as our "fight-or-flight" mechanism, which activates in response to stress, mobilizing our body to face immediate challenges. The parasympathetic system is responsible for calming the body after a stress response, bringing the body back to a balanced state.

What psychologists have discovered is that we operate most optimally in situations where these two subsystems function in appropriate balance. Specifically, psychologists have found that we do want some activation of the sympathetic nervous system to help us feel challenged and engaged, but not so much that we move into a state of hyperarousal, where we lose control over our cognitions and emotions in a fight-or-flight response. We also do not want our parasympathetic nervous system to overactivate. When this happens, we move into a state of hypoarousal, where we enter a freeze or submission response and disengage cognitively and emotionally.

The optimal band of emotional arousal is our window of tolerance. When you're within your window of tolerance, you can think clearly, manage your emotions, and respond to challenges in a balanced way. But if pushed outside of this range, you may feel overwhelmed and out of control, leading to either heightened anxiety or emotional numbness.

The reality is that some people have narrower windows of tolerance, meaning it is easier for them to lose control of their cognitions and emotions when faced with stress. Other people have wide windows of tolerance, meaning they can take on significant stress without any loss of control. In fact, the width of this window is a decent way to assess our altitude along our Being Side. The wider it is, the greater our Being Side altitude.

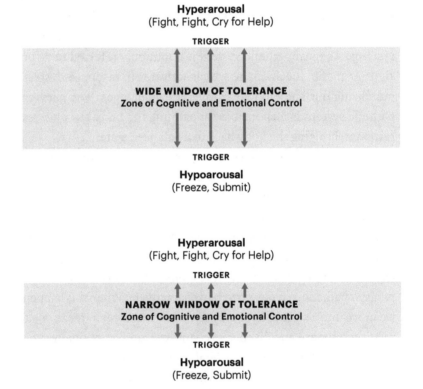

The famous boxer Mike Tyson once said, "Everyone has a plan until they get punched in the mouth." This quote taps into the concept of our window of tolerance. When we operate within our window of tolerance, we do a better job of sticking to our plans and our intentions to create value. But if we get figuratively, or maybe even literally, punched in the mouth, we lose connection to our plans and intentions and enter self-protection mode, where we operate from a place of reaction.

I believe that people are more inclined to operate as value creators when they are in contexts that are stress-free and where they feel safe because they are likely operating within their window of tolerance. But a question arises: How much does it take for us to be thrown out of our window of tolerance and move toward more self-protective operating? The width of our window of tolerance is an indicator of the percentage of our time that we spend as value creators as opposed to self-protectors. Those with a narrow window of tolerance are sent into reactive self-protection mode much more quickly and more often than those with wide windows of tolerance.

Think about my son's athletic coach. He is generally a nice guy. But he clearly has a narrow window of tolerance for his players making mistakes. So, when his players make mistakes, he easily loses cognitive and emotional control and engages in reactive behaviors that are inappropriate for the context.

And think about Brené Brown. Can you sense how a foundational aspect of her *becoming better* upgrade involved widening her window of tolerance for silence and vulnerability?

What I have come to learn is that the people who create the most value in their world also have the widest windows of tolerance.

The width of our window of tolerance is an indicator of the percentage of our time that we spend as value creators as opposed to self-protectors.

———————————————

Bringing These Four Insights Together

To bring these four insights together, consider the following example: getting cut off when driving.

When drivers with narrow windows of tolerance get cut off on the road, they generally make meaning of it as a personal attack and quickly move to a state of dysregulation where they lose control of their emotions and enter a fit of rage. And they generally feel very justified in their reaction. In fact, I recently got the double-bird from someone while I was merging into a lane. I am not sure one flips the double-bird from within one's window of tolerance.

But when drivers with wide windows of tolerance get cut off, they do not take it as a personal attack, which allows them to hold strong and unpleasant emotions at bay. They stay more balanced and regulated, allowing them to navigate the situation more effectively in the moment, perhaps by backing off and creating a safe distance between them and the other driver. And the benefits extend beyond the moment. Many people who lose their cool in these situations carry their emotions with them well after the event. Those who are able to keep their cool will have a greater capacity to operate as a value creator into the near future.

Unfortunately, this is more than just a laughing matter. In my community, there was a situation where a mom accidentally cut off a person on the local freeway. This sent one of the individuals in the cut-off vehicle outside of his window of tolerance to the degree that he did something I doubt he would have done within it: He pulled out a gun and shot a bullet into the rear of the vehicle. What he did not know was that there was a car seat in the back, and his bullet struck the back of the child sitting in the seat, killing him. This was surely an emotional reaction meant to make him, the shooter, feel better, but it clearly led to an outcome that is the opposite of value-creating.

It's a tragic example. But I believe it illustrates a key lesson of this book. Most of the time when we misstep, it is not because of a lack of knowledge and skills; it is because of deficiencies along our Being Side. I personally believe that shooter knew better and had the skills to do better. But I also believe the shooter had a Being Side that was unsophisticated and unrefined.

Key Discoveries

There are three central lessons to take from this chapter:

1 The altitude of our Being Side is the degree to which our internal operating system is wired for value creation versus self-protection.

2 Two ways you can start to evaluate the altitude of your Being Side are by investigating the quality of your meaning-making and the width of your window of tolerance.

3 What makes this evaluation of our Being Side altitude challenging is that our self-protective programming feels right and justifiable to us.

Keep in mind, developmental psychologists have found that if we have a lineup of 100 adults taken from the general population, 64 of them will operate at a low Being Side altitude with strong self-protective meaning-making tendencies and narrow windows of tolerance; 35 will be in the middle of the lineup with a moderate Being Side altitude; and only one of them will operate at a high altitude with strong value-creating meaning-making tendencies and a wide window of tolerance. Essentially all of us have room to upgrade our internal operating systems and become more wired for value creation, myself included.

Applications for Leadership

Just as most people have Being Side deficiencies, so do leaders. From my experience, it is common for leaders to possess narrow windows of tolerance for risk, uncertainty, and vulnerability, and thus make meaning of them as things to be avoided. While this protects them from experiencing discomfort in the short term, it ultimately limits their ability to be an effective leader who creates meaningful value in the present and in the future.

In fact, understanding this has led me to recognize that the Being Side altitude of leaders sets the ceiling for the organizations and groups that they lead.

When leaders operate from a low Being Side altitude, they institute policies, practices, and cultures that inject self-protection into the system and limit value creation. For example, if an employee makes a mistake, leaders with low Being Side altitudes might formalize a policy to help ensure that mistake doesn't occur in the future. While that new policy might make the leader feel more safe and secure, it generally institutes a level of bureaucracy that impedes empowerment and agility.

But here is the good news: Leaders can elevate along their Being Side. They can upgrade their internal operating system such that they improve their meaning-making and expand their window of tolerance. When they do so, they raise the ceiling of the organization and groups that they lead. This is because with a wider window of tolerance and more value-creating programming, they will institute transformational changes to improve the culture and processes of the organization. Oftentimes that involves a shift from bureaucracy to greater empowerment.

In fact, I dare you to find a company that transformationally elevated their organization and long-term value-creating abilities without its leaders elevating along their Being Side, either through development or replacement. And when you see organizations take a step down or backwards, I encourage you to explore if that is because they brought in leaders who operate at a lower Being Side altitude. Two excellent case studies to consider are Microsoft and Boeing. I'll let you determine which one shifted toward value creation and which one shifted toward self-protection.

4

Primary Causes of Being Side Differences

*The new midlife is where you realize that even your
failures make you more beautiful and are turned spiritually
into success if you became a better person because of them.*

MARIANNE WILLIAMSON

WHEN I START coaching a leader, I try to determine two things as early as possible. The first is the altitude of that leader's Being Side. I pay attention to cues about the quality of their meaning-making, their window of tolerance, and other factors we'll cover in upcoming chapters. By determining where they are at, I get a sense of the person I am working with and what messages might connect most powerfully with them.

While this is a necessary foundation to establish, it is not enough to start mapping the optimal route to a higher Being Side altitude.

So the second thing I try to determine is the reason (or reasons) they are at their current Being Side altitude and not a higher one. Is there something that is keeping them at their current altitude, something that is restricting them from elevating? If I can get a clear answer to this question, I can more effectively map their journey from their current Being Side altitude to a higher altitude.

Through my research and my experience working with leaders, I have found there are three broad buckets of factors that impact our altitude along our Being Side and explain why our internal operating system might be more programmed for self-protection versus value creation. In this chapter, I will identify and discuss these factors at a high level. We'll dive deeper into them later in the book as we get into awakening to our current Being Side altitude (part 2) and upgrading ourselves to operate at a higher level (part 3).

The Three Big Factors That Impact Our Being Side Altitude

The three factors that play a significant role in our self-protective wiring and constrain our Being Side development are traumatic life experiences, unhealthy cultures, and our neurological functionality.

Through my personal experience as well as that from coaching leaders, I have made several observations related to these three factors. The first is that if someone has self-protective wiring built into their internal operating system, which is essentially all of us, then they have been negatively impacted by at least one of these factors. I have yet to find an exception to this.

The second observation is that since the way our internal operating system operates feels right, good, and justifiable to us, most people do not fully recognize or appreciate the role these factors have played and continue to play in their lives. For example, most people have experienced trauma to the degree that it has impacted their Being Side altitude, yet not many are willing to acknowledge their past trauma, nor are they aware of how that past trauma shows up in how they operate today. And similarly, Len Adler, a leading researcher on ADHD, reports that at least 75 percent of adults who have ADHD do not know they have it.

The third observation is that the more one can recognize and appreciate the role these factors play in their lives, the more they are willing and able to do the deep work of upgrading their internal operating system and transformationally *become better*.

Let's just say I learned this the hard way. I'll tell the story in greater detail later, but there was a time when I reached out to a trauma therapist to explore doing some Being Side development. The first thing I said to her was, "I don't think I have trauma in my background, but I want to try out a developmental technique that you specialize in."

The reality was that, at the time, I was unaware of and in denial of trauma in my past. But when I started working with my therapist, she pointed out that some of my upbringing was not normal and identified a variety of signs and signals that my internal operating system was not functioning as optimally as it could. And now, having worked on my past trauma, I can confidently state that I would not have been able to transformationally elevate along my Being Side without awakening to my trauma, owning it, and working through it.

So if you have trauma in your past, operate in an unhealthy environment, or have neurological functionality issues, I don't want you to run from that. I want you to create space to explore these things, which we will do in part 2. But for now, sit back while I explain how these factors play a role in our Being Side altitude.

Factor 1: Traumatic Life Experiences

Imagine that your body is a bucket that collects drops of life experiences. Most of these drops are small and clear, representing normal day-to-day experiences. But some drops might take on different colors. For example, a happy experience might take on a light blue coloration, while a painful experience might take on black. And some drops might be larger and more significant than others.

The simple truth is that this collection of our life's experiences has come to shape our Being Side altitude. While most drops will not likely pollute the entire bucket, if you get enough drops or larger drops of one color, the water will take on a particular color tone. This can impact your window of tolerance and how you make meaning of your world. For example, if all you have experienced is pain and poverty, the coloration in which you see the world is going to be vastly different from someone who grew up experiencing well-being and abundance.

I'll highlight three examples to demonstrate how our traumatic past experiences can shape how our internal operating system is programmed to see and interact with our present world.

Example 1. My wife's experience watching the scary clown movie *It* when she was three was formative enough that it has impacted how she sees and experiences clowns as an adult. Her internal operating system is now programmed to make meaning of clowns as a threat, so she possesses a narrower window of tolerance related to clowns than most people. And when she sees a clown, she easily gets "triggered" and quickly moves into self-protection mode.

Example 2. Consider my dad. For half of his career, from about 1960 to 1983, my dad was an entrepreneur. He ran a small civil engineering company. In the early 1980s, he went through a string of difficulties. His wife at the time lost her battle with cancer, leaving him as the single parent of three teenagers. He quickly remarried and struggled to integrate his new wife as the teens' stepmom. The United States fell into an economic recession, significantly affecting his business. And, shortly thereafter, I was born.

These events made for a "perfect storm" that I think was too much for him. Now, of course, I did not know him before these events occurred, but from what I am told, he became a rather different person.

One of the ways this was manifest was in his relationship and window of tolerance with risk. During the first half of his career, he seemed to have at least an "okay" relationship with it. He clearly was willing to take risks as an entrepreneur. But after these events, his relationship with risk took a nosedive, and he became extremely risk-averse.

Shortly after I was born, he decided to sell his stake in his business and get a civic job with one of the larger cities in northern Utah. This was a position with a lot of stability but very few opportunities for advancement and increased pay.

Throughout my upbringing, I was admonished by my father and taught that taking risks is scary, debt is bad, and being an entrepreneur can put your family at risk. Additionally, my parents, in my opinion, were excessively frugal with money.

Looking back, I think it is easy to see that my father's string of difficult, even traumatic, experiences altered his window of tolerance related to risk. These tough experiences left him more wired for safety, security, and self-protection. While his heightened sensitivity to risk makes sense in hindsight and is justifiable, it was a shift that was not only personally limiting but had a huge impact on those around him, primarily my mother and me. And, being raised under his influence, I entered adulthood with a mindset about risk, debt, and entrepreneurship that I ultimately found limiting.

Example 3. Let's dive more fully into the idea that our relationships with our primary caregivers as children can impact our window of tolerance and meaning-making. A great theory to explain this is attachment theory. I've talked a little about attachment styles already, but let's go deeper.

Attachment theory suggests that the quality of our emotional bonds with our primary caregivers as children impacts the degree to which our internal operating system allows us to form relationships and operate healthily in those relationships as adults. In fact, these researchers have identified four different attachment styles, or patterns of operation within relationships, that range from more healthy to less healthy based on the quality of our childhood bonds.

The highest-quality attachment style is a secure attachment style, which is the result of high-quality childhood bonds. When people have a secure attachment style, they are programmed to be more trusting of their world and their relationship partners. They feel safe to explore and engage in the world around them without the assistance of others. And, when they enter relationships, they are trusting that their partners will meet their needs and provide support when necessary. They have stronger emotional regulation skills and are generally good at expressing their emotions and needs as part of their emotional regulation process, making them more resilient and easier to connect with. They also have a healthy self-image. They see themselves as being of value and worth, leading to positive self-esteem. All of these elements make it so that their nervous system is not anxious or scared when they enter relationships and remain in them. This also allows them to have a wider window of tolerance for potential slights from their partner or challenges in their relationship.

Lower-quality attachment styles include anxious and avoidant styles. People who have these styles generally did not have a high-quality connection with their primary caregiver as a child, resulting in them being more fearful of abandonment (anxious) or of intimacy (avoidant).

People who have an anxious attachment style are often insecure in their relationships. They are wired to seek consistent expressions of love and commitment, and they struggle with independence and time apart from their partner. Because of their anxious insecurity, they have a narrow window of tolerance for any signals that might indicate that their partner is going to leave them. Their internal operating system even interprets normal, healthy behaviors, like their partner going out with friends, as a signal that they are not loved or wanted.

People who have an avoidant attachment style are uncomfortable with relationships. They are wired for independence, are prone to struggle with commitment, fear vulnerability, and are generally not very emotionally expressive. Because of their need for independence, they have a narrow window of tolerance for intimacy and closeness in a romantic relationship. As a result, their internal operating system often interprets normal, healthy behaviors incorrectly. For example, they might see healthy bids for affection or emotional expressions by their partner as a trap to reduce their independence, or their partner being "needy."

The lowest-quality attachment style is the disorganized style. People with a disorganized attachment style generally had unhealthy relationships with their primary caregivers as children and carry both anxious and avoidant tendencies, making them quite erratic in their relationships. For example, they will commonly feel torn between wanting emotional closeness while also fearing it, which can make them "hot" one moment but very "cold" and distant the next. They are generally not trusting of others and will often operate in a manner that prevents others from trusting them. As a result, they are prone to seek partners that perpetuate a cycle of emotional turmoil and instability.

In my own journey, I have learned that my default attachment style is an avoidant style. So part of my personal development has focused on rewiring my internal operating system to develop more of a secure attachment style.

Across my coaching clients, as we dive into their leadership struggles, they will commonly connect their unhealthy leadership tendencies back to their childhood and how they were raised. For

There is no finish
line to our *being better*
development path.

———————————————

example, I was once coaching Paul, an executive in a mid-sized financial institution, and we surfaced that one of his struggles was that he found it hard to take initiative. He could effectively lead when told what to do, but he struggled to come up with what to do without someone telling him. When I asked him why he thought taking initiative was so difficult for him, he immediately spoke of his relationship with his father. He said, "Growing up, I could never please my dad, no matter what I did. So I was always seeking his approval. Even now, as a grown man, I feel like I need to ask for his permission before making a big decision, like buying a new car."

As you can sense, because of his upbringing Paul has developed an anxious attachment style that makes him reluctant to take initiative out of fear that he might disappoint his boss, the CEO. So a big part of my coaching Paul was focused on helping him develop new and upgraded programming to take greater initiative. While he has made some transformational improvements, I don't feel his work is yet done. And, to me, that is a reminder that there is no finish line to our *being better* development path.

Across all three of these examples, there is a primary lesson to learn: The more trauma we experience, the more our bodies become programmed for self-protection. It is a natural adjustment our nervous system makes to help ensure that we stay safe.

Factor 2: Current Culture

Not only do our traumatic life experiences impact our Being Side altitude, but so does our present culture. If someone steps into a new situation or setting that involves high pressure, reduced safety, and/or self-protective norms, that new setting is likely to negatively impact their internal operating system and window of tolerance, causing them to move toward self-protection and away from value creation.

For example, if a person who is normally very creative gets a job at a company that does not tolerate failure or mistakes, the cultural pressure to avoid mistakes will cause the new employee to increasingly narrow their window of tolerance for failure. In turn, this will negatively impact their creativity, at least in that setting.

I experienced this personally when I made a temporary transition from academia to consulting and worked for Gallup for a year. In academia, professors do not have to bill their hours to any clients. This helps foster an environment where it is easy to collaborate with colleagues. So I was used to bringing forward unpolished creative ideas to my colleagues and seeking their input to improve those ideas. But when I started working at Gallup, where consultants have to bill their hours to their clients, I found that my colleagues were not willing to collaborate and consult with me. Because of the incentive structure involved in the billing process, any minute spent brainstorming with me was a minute working that they couldn't bill. In fact, in one of my initial attempts to be creative, I brought a half-baked idea to the highest-ranking consultant in the office, hoping to get his insights and recommendations for bringing the idea to life. Instead of engaging in a collaborative discussion, I was reprimanded for not working out all the kinks before presenting the idea.

Through this experience, and after becoming accustomed to the client billing process, over the 10 months I was at Gallup I realized that I was not my old collaborative and creative self. Instead, I now had a narrow window of tolerance for operating in creativity mode and was rather unwilling to collaborate and innovate with others because, like them, I had become solely focused on doing work that could be billed back to the client.

This personal experience is something I have seen played out in hundreds of organizations: The quality of an organization's culture has a direct effect on the quality of employees' internal operating systems. In general, cultures that are competitive, high-pressured, and psychologically unsafe lead to a narrowing of one's window of tolerance and the development of a more self-protective and less sophisticated internal operating system. But cultures that are collaborative, balanced, and psychologically safe provide the opportunity for people to widen their windows of tolerance and develop more value-creating and sophisticated operating systems.

In fact, the most remarkable business transformations involve leaders who, because they operate at a high Being Side altitude, were able to elevate their organization's culture from being competitive and high-pressured to being collaborative and psychologically safe, such as Alan Mulally at Ford and Satya Nadella at Microsoft. In both of these instances, these leaders prioritized the development of value-creating cultures that helped their employees adopt more value-creating internal operating systems. This was an essential key to these leaders dramatically improving their organizations' performance, success, and ability to create value for nearly all of their stakeholders.

And, while I have leveraged my experience in organizations here, I have also seen and experienced how the power of culture exists in homes, families, religions, and professional associations. The reality is that any social group's culture impacts the programming of its members' internal operating systems.

Factor 3: Neurological Functionality

In addition to our experiences, our Being Side can be impacted by genetic factors, injuries, or illnesses that alter our neurological functionality. Whole books could be written on just this topic, and many have been. But for brevity, let me demonstrate this by using the example of ADHD.

ADHD is a relatively common neurodevelopmental disorder that affects the quality and sophistication of one's executive functioning. Those with ADHD have neurological deficiencies that cause them to have a more heightened stress response system and a narrower window of tolerance, making it easier for them to be neurologically programmed for self-protection as opposed to value creation.

For example, people with ADHD struggle particularly with two groups of behaviors: (1) persisting toward goals while resisting distractions, and (2) inhibiting impulsive actions. In fact, research suggests that people with ADHD fall approximately 30 percent behind non-ADHD people in these abilities. This means their internal operating system is (1) more programmed for self-protection, such that they are more prone to seek out activities that bring benefits and pleasure to them in the short term, and (2) less programmed for value-creating tasks such as making a game plan, staying on task, thinking efficiently, and choosing what's important to pay attention to.

Despite these challenges, a great many people and leaders with ADHD are still able to be effective and successful. In fact, it is common for people with ADHD to use some of these challenges to their advantage. But nonetheless, these neurological deficiencies do impact the overall quality, functionality, and sophistication of one's internal operating system.

The good news about ADHD is that effective treatments and self-regulation strategies exist that can be engaged in to limit ADHD's hindering role in one's Being Side altitude. But unfortunately, there are other neurological conditions or factors that impact our Being Side and may not be treated as easily, such as Parkinson's disease or dementia.

Since ADHD is one of the most common neurological disorders that affect our internal operating system, we'll dive more deeply into its role in one's Being Side altitude in chapter 15.

Key Discoveries

There are three primary factors that cause our internal operating system to become more wired for self-protection as opposed to value creation. They are:

- traumatic life experiences
- toxic or unhealthy cultures
- issues that impact our neurological functionality

Unfortunately, it is likely that all of us have been impacted by at least one of these three things. Consider these statistics:

- The National Council for Mental Wellbeing reports that 70 percent of adults have experienced some type of traumatic event at least once in their life.

- *The Muse* reports that 64 percent of people have faced toxic situations at work.

- In an article published by the *British Medical Bulletin*, neurodiversity researcher Dr. Nancy Doyle reports that 15 to 20 percent of people are neurodivergent.

Because of our normal maturation as people, along with these factors, we all have some self-protective wiring. This suggests that we all have some reprogramming to do if we want to *become better*. I'll introduce how we can do that in the next chapter.

Applications for Leadership

When I work with organizations, my usual point of contact is the head of human resources. I have observed some human resources leaders who understand and appreciate the impact traumatic experiences, culture, and neurological conditions can have on their organizations' leaders and employees, and others who do not. Let me compare and contrast these two types of human resources leaders and the differences in how they think about leadership development when they are working with a leader who is struggling in their position.

The human resources leaders who do not understand these concepts generally approach their struggling leaders as if they are lacking or broken. Their strategy is to send them to a coach or development program to help them gain more knowledge or skills in an effort to to "fix" them.

But the human resources leaders who do understand these concepts think about their struggling leaders very differently. In fact, in a recent conversation I was talking with a human resources leader who is well aware of these Being Side principles. We were discussing a struggling leader in her organization. The HR person, who I'll call Jennifer, said to me, "This leader is limited in her effectiveness because she has insecurities that cause her to focus too strongly on driving results and not focus enough on connecting with and unifying her leadership team."

And then, in a compassionate way, Jennifer wondered out loud, "I wonder what has happened in her past that has led her to be this insecure. Is it something related to trauma, or is it because she was so strongly influenced by the culture of her prior organization?"

From this conversation, I could tell that this human resources leader didn't see the struggling leader as a problem to be fixed, but as a person to be cared for.

If you are a leader who wants to show up at a higher level, consider:

- Are there past hurts that I need to heal from?

- Are there cultural barriers that are influencing my body's need to be self-protective?

- Do I have any neurological deficiencies that I need to get support for?

5

How to Elevate Along Your Being Side

Sometimes, what you want is already waiting for you, alongside the person that you are capable of becoming.

C. JOYBELL C.

ONE OF THE CLEAREST lessons I have learned through my personal *becoming better* efforts, as well as from helping thousands through the process of *becoming better*, is that we all have some self-protective wiring. While this wiring serves us by helping us feel more safe, comfortable, and protected, it is also holding us back from being a better, more impactful version of ourselves.

Let me give you some common examples of such self-protective wiring among the leaders and people I have worked with.

Bruno is a vice president who leads through control rather than empowerment, and he struggles to listen to his team. Why? Because his operating system is programmed with several interrelated and limiting beliefs. First, he believes that his way is the best way to do things. Second, he believes that if the work does not get done his way, solutions will not be implemented fast enough. And third, he believes that if solutions are not implemented quickly, he will not be valued. These three beliefs are a strong indicator that his internal wiring is set up to protect his perceived value. As a result, he engages in controlling leadership, not to create value for those he leads but to help him feel safer, more comfortable, and valued. Interestingly, Bruno thought his style of leadership was optimal and high-quality. It wasn't until I started working with him that he began to awaken to his self-protective programming and see that his leadership was causing collateral damage to his team.

Vicki is a single woman who wants to have more success in her dating life and hopes to find a lifelong partner. Unfortunately, she has struggled to develop close relationships with those she has dated. As we dug into this, we discovered that she struggles to open herself up and be vulnerable by sharing her opinions and feelings with those she dates. She identified a self-protective belief when she said, "I have a belief that if I share my opinions and feelings with those I date, then my dating partners will judge me, make me feel bad, or reject me." The irony of this limiting belief lies in its purpose: it is designed to shield her from emotional rejection, yet by keeping her from opening up and fostering genuine connection, it ensures the very rejection she fears.

And recall Sheryl from the Introduction, the woman who has a number of degrees and certificates and was frustrated because she was continuing to get passed over for promotion into a leadership role? What we discovered when I worked with her was that her internal operating system carried a belief that if she made a mistake, misstepped, or caused a problem, she would lose her job, something she needed as a single mother. Being programmed in this way, she was reluctant to take initiative. While not taking initiative helped her to feel more safe and secure, it ultimately was preventing her from being seen as someone her organization could trust to fill a leadership role.

You and I may not be programmed in these exact same ways, but we each have our own self-protective wiring. And whether it is any of these three people, or you or me, we are going to have to rise above our self-protective wiring if we are going to transformationally *become better*.

Thus far, we have discussed the *becoming better* process and journey in three ways, all meaning the same thing:

- elevating along our Being Side
- upgrading our body's internal operating system
- healing, refining, and improving our body's nervous system

Regardless of how we communicate the *becoming better* process, you should more fully recognize that doing this type of self-improvement work differs from traditional and typical development efforts focused on improving along our Doing Side by gaining greater knowledge and skills. These efforts require a different form of development.

Two Types of Development

There are two different ways we can develop ourselves. Let's now put formal labels on these two forms of development.

The first form is called horizontal development. It involves developing ourselves along our Doing Side by improving our knowledge, skills, and abilities. I called this the "*doing better* developmental path" in the Introduction.

The second is called vertical development, which focuses on our Being Side. It involves developing ourselves by upgrading our internal operating system. I called this the "*being better* developmental path" in the Introduction.

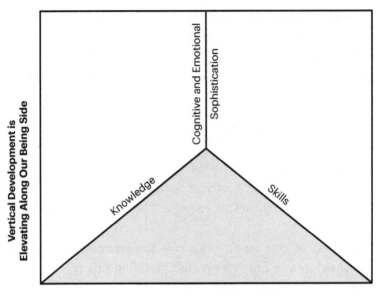

**Horizontal Development is
Expanding Along Our Doing Side**

Horizontal development is a process that is similar to downloading apps onto an iPad. The new apps broaden the iPad's functionality and allow it to do more than what it could do previously. But horizontal development has a huge limitation: Adding a new app onto ourselves does not necessarily improve how effectively our internal operating system functions. There are many people who, like Sheryl, have downloaded very advanced apps through training and degree programs. But they are unable to fully employ them because their operating system is not sophisticated enough to operate them.

We are all intimately familiar with horizontal development. Think about your high school or college classes. Their primary focus is to download knowledge and skills onto your personal iPad so that you can do more than you could previously. For example, if you take an accounting class, you learn how to do accounting things. While this might help you land an accounting job, it does not improve your ability to make meaning of your world in more effective and elevated ways or widen your window of tolerance, allowing you to more effectively navigate the stress and complexity that will come with that accounting job.

If we want to elevate our capacity to navigate the challenges, stress, and complexity of our world, we need vertical development.

Unfortunately, very few development efforts involve vertical development. Thus, most people are not very familiar with the concept.

So let's make sure we clearly define and understand what vertical development is. I am going to unveil two definitions, one technical and the other rephrased from the foundation we have laid. Both definitions mean the same thing.

The technical definition of vertical development is: elevating our ability to make meaning of our world in more cognitively and emotionally sophisticated ways.

But here is perhaps a clearer way to define it: elevating our internal operating system's ability to interpret, process, and respond to our world in value-creating ways as opposed to self-protective ways.

A comparison of these definitions reveals that people with greater cognitive and emotional sophistication have the capacity to (1) suspend instinctual self-protective reactions, which allows them to (2) process and operate in more value-creating ways.

I have given several examples of vertical development thus far. For example, I upgraded my internal operating system from being afraid of starting up a business (i.e., self-protective wiring) to being willing to become an entrepreneur as a way to open up desired possibilities for myself and my family (i.e., value-creating wiring). And Brené Brown upgraded her internal operating system from being resistant to vulnerability (self-protective wiring) to accepting and welcoming it so that she could be more courageous and live more wholeheartedly (value-creating wiring).

The Two Primary Benefits of Vertical Development

When we vertically develop, we are improving ourselves at our most foundational level. We are refining how our body makes sense of and processes information. And that changes everything! It changes how we think, how we learn, and how we behave.

As an example, consider how the altitude of one's Being Side impacts how they respond to constructive criticism. When someone who is less vertically developed receives constructive criticism, they move toward self-protection and get defensive, which causes them to think about the feedback negatively, not learn from it, and dismiss it. But if that person is able to vertically develop, create a wider window of tolerance for constructive criticism, and make meaning of it as being helpful for their learning and growth, they will think about it more positively, learn from it, and approach it. Not only will this shift help them in the moment of receiving constructive criticism, but can you see how it will lead to a completely different developmental trajectory for the rest of their life?

Another benefit of vertical development is that it helps us more effectively utilize our Doing Side knowledge, skills, and abilities. If you take two people whose Doing Side capabilities are at the same level, the person with a higher Being Side altitude will employ them more effectively and in more value-creating ways. For example, there are many baseball players that have elite-level skills along their Doing Side. But what seems to set the best baseball players apart from the rest is that they have Being Side abilities to withstand stress, bounce back after failure, and continually push themselves to learn.

An example of this is Billy Beane of *Moneyball* fame. As a player coming out of high school, he was identified as one of the most skilled prospects. But despite his skills, he was unsuccessful professionally because of his inability to withstand the pressure of playing in the major leagues and be resilient in responding to his batting

Definition of Vertical Development:
Elevating our internal operating
system's ability to interpret, process,
and respond to our world in more
value-creating ways as opposed
to self-protective ways.

———————————————

struggles. There are many baseball players who have had less skill than Billy Beane but had better baseball careers. This is because they were more developed on their Being Side.

But to give him credit, Beane seemed to be able to vertically develop somewhere in his journey from baseball player to general manager of the Oakland Athletics. As a general manager, he demonstrated that he was more wired for creating value than for self-protection by his willingness to put his job on the line by taking a new and radical approach to player selection based on analytics. His willingness to go beyond typical player-selection conventions allowed him to put together a championship-contending team despite having one of the lowest payrolls in baseball.

As we continue through this book, I'll give you more examples of these benefits of vertical development.

But here is the reality: If you are going to *become better*, it will have to involve vertical development.

Key Discoveries

The introductory chapters in this book started with the premise that if we want to transformationally *become better*, we need to take three steps:

1 understanding what our Being Side is
2 awakening to the current quality of our Being Side
3 elevating along our Being Side

We have now wrapped up step number one. You should now feel like you have clarity on what your Being Side is and why it needs to be the focus of your *becoming better* development.

And, in this chapter, we put a label to this form of development: vertical development.

Later I'll give you direction on how you can vertically develop (step number three). But before we get into that, it is important that you next take step two in your *becoming better* journey: awakening to the current quality of your *being* (i.e., your Being Side altitude).

When I started to awaken to my Being Side altitude, I found I had vastly overestimated how high it was. I didn't have much self-awareness of my self-protective programming and how it was holding me back.

As I came to learn more and more about my Being Side, I could more clearly see that I had more work to do on it than I'd anticipated. While this was humbling, it set me on a journey that I never could have expected, a journey that has proven to be life-changing, life-elevating, and transformational.

I want the same outcomes for you.

Applications for Leadership

As discussed earlier, 7 percent of leaders operate from a low Being Side altitude, 85 percent from a moderate altitude, and 8 percent from a high altitude. There are several reasons why I think this is, but I'll focus on a couple here.

First, when leaders shift from a low to a moderate Being Side altitude, they recognize that they do operate at an elevated level compared to most people, and they might assume they have "arrived" and are not in need of further development.

Second, leaders I work with commonly tell me, "I am not sure I have ever met or worked with a leader that operates from a high Being Side altitude." What they are saying is that they have never had a good role model of what it means to operate from a high Being Side altitude. And if a leader doesn't have a vertically developed role model to look up to, they may not recognize that they aren't yet where they could be.

Putting these two reasons together, my experience working with leaders has taught me that very few have even thought about awakening to the self-protective tendencies that may be preventing them from being greater value creators. As a result, few have ever given vertical development much emphasis.

So let me prompt you to give it greater emphasis. Consider:

- Do you believe there is room for you to operate from a higher Being Side altitude?

- Do you have any role models that operate from a high Being Side altitude?

- Do you need to prioritize vertical development more in your life?

PART TWO

To Become Better, You Must Awaken to the Quality and Sophistication of Your Being Side

6

Deepen Your Self-Awareness

Who I am to be, I am now becoming.
BENJAMIN FRANKLIN

WELCOME TO STEP NUMBER TWO: awakening to the quality of your Being Side. This step is all about self-awareness, something that research has determined is easier said than done.

Tasha Eurich, a self-awareness researcher, has conducted research to answer two thought-provoking questions. Try to guess the answer she found to each.

Question 1: How many people think they are self-aware?

Question 2: How many people are actually self-aware?

Eurich has found that almost everyone—95 percent—thinks they are self-aware. But only 10-15 percent are actually self-aware. Eurich states that this means "80 percent of us are lying to ourselves about whether we're lying to ourselves."

How do we make sense of this huge disconnect?

Let's start by defining what self-awareness is. Then, let's connect the concept of self-awareness to what we have learned about our internal operating system. In doing so, you'll get clarity about why most people are not as self-aware as they think.

One of my favorite definitions of self-awareness comes from Stephen R. Covey, who is best known for writing *The 7 Habits of Highly Effective People*. He defines self-awareness as the ability "to stand apart from ourselves and examine our thinking, our motives, our history, our scripts, our actions, and our habits and tendencies."

Based on what we have covered thus far in this book, which side of ourselves controls and determines the elements he mentions: our Doing Side or Being Side? It is our internal operating system associated with our Being Side.

I think most people believe they are self-aware because they know their Doing Side knowledge, skills, and abilities. But most people do not have a deep awareness of the programming associated with their internal operating system and the degree to which they are wired for self-protection versus value creation. And what makes self-awareness especially difficult is whether we are programmed for self-protection or value creation, such programming feels right and good to us. Thus, many do not feel the need to deeply inspect it.

Two Examples of a Lack of Self-Awareness

I want to share with you how uncommon it is for people to be self-aware by identifying two people who had thought they were self-aware but only recently came to realize that they were less so than they had originally believed: Me and my wife, Jena.

Deepening My Self-Awareness

Let's start with me. A few years ago, I read a book that really helped me understand that people have an internal operating system that is (1) connected to our nervous system, (2) largely resides below the level of our consciousness, and (3) influences almost everything we do. Titled *The Body Keeps the Score* by Bessel van der Kolk, the book is all about how the trauma we experience in life alters how effectively our body functions cognitively, emotionally, and physically. We'll dive more into the connection between trauma and our internal operating system in chapter 14. But for now, recall that when a person experiences trauma, their body rewires its internal operating system to become more self-protective. While this is a natural and possibly life-saving adaptation, such wiring can be limiting in our journey to become the best version of ourselves.

When I read this book, I honestly felt I had not experienced trauma in my life. But the more I learned about trauma and its effects, I could not deny that I operated with many of the signs of someone who had experienced it. The sign that resonated the most with me was a term I was not familiar with: dissociation. Dissociation is a mental and emotional condition where a person has a difficult time connecting with their feelings and emotions, and in extreme cases, their senses, memories, and sense of identity. For me, I recognized that my internal operating system was wired to stay in my cognitions and to steer away from the feelings and emotions in my body.

As I learned about dissociation, it was the first time I recognized that how I experience the world may not be how most people experience it, and may not be the best way either.

So, when Bessel van der Kolk wrote about the various treatment options for healing from past trauma and becoming less dissociated, I paid extra attention.

One trauma-treatment modality that I found particularly interesting was a form of therapy called EMDR, which stands for Eye Movement Desensitization and Reprocessing. When therapists use this technique, they have their patient engage with bilateral stimulation in the form of side-to-side eye movements, pings in the ears, tapping, or hand buzzers. And while the patient is engaging with these stimulations, the therapist guides the patient into exploring their blocks and past traumas. Interestingly, EMDR researchers and practitioners have found that, for reasons we do not fully understand, these bilateral stimulations allow a patient to step into distressing memories and reprocess them without experiencing much emotional intensity. It has been shown to be among the most helpful forms of therapy for fostering psychological healing from trauma.

Intrigued by the power of EMDR, I reached out to a local therapist who specialized in it. When we first connected, I told her I had just learned that I might struggle with dissociation, but I was quick to add that I didn't think I had trauma in my background. I am sure she chuckled on the inside when I gave that qualifier, but she went on to tell me that regardless of the source of my dissociation, she felt EMDR could help me out.

So, I began working with her. We started with a combination of EMDR and another form of therapy, called Internal Family Systems Therapy, that helps you awaken to and connect with different parts of yourself.

From this experience, I learned three big lessons.

The first lesson probably wasn't a shock to my therapist, but it was to me. I came to learn that I *did* have trauma in my past. While I had never been abused, I learned I had been emotionally neglected by my parents throughout my upbringing. Until then, I had thought my upbringing was normal. But when we started to dive into some difficult times during my childhood, I realized that my parents never expressed love, care, or nurturing to me in those difficult times, and that not receiving such love, care, and nurturing was not normal or healthy.

The second lesson I learned came from the Internal Family Systems Therapy. Specifically, as I started to connect more deeply with myself, I came to feel that my whole "me" was made up of different parts of myself that play different roles in my life. Some of these parts were younger versions of myself that were connected to specific and more extreme instances of emotional neglect. I also learned I had built up other parts of myself, called "protectors," to guard these more vulnerable areas. The more I got in touch with these parts of myself, the more I came to realize that my protectors played a dominant role in my internal operating system and how I operated across the different domains of my life. And one of the primary roles that my protectors played was to hold me back from connecting with my feelings and emotions.

By connecting my childhood neglect to my self-protective tendencies, I could now clearly see how my past has played a big role in how I show up in my present. When I was a child, I was on my own to meet my own emotional needs. And the best way for my 10-year-old self to deal with emotional discomfort was to allow my protectors to step in and block the negative feelings that were trying to arise.

This avoidance of my negative and hurt feelings as a child was my nervous system's way of protecting me. And while it did a great job of protecting me in challenging situations as a child, it ingrained the programming patterns of dissociation that were restraining my Being Side altitude as an adult.

The third lesson I learned going through this therapy process was that I largely operated with an avoidant attachment style.

Because of the emotional neglect I experienced in childhood, my internal operating system developed self-protective programming that made me extremely independent. My operating system did not want me to put myself in positions similar to my childhood, where I had to rely on someone else to meet my needs and then have them neglect those needs. So in my relationships, even my relationship with my wife, I have learned that my operating system struggles with vulnerability, reliance on others, and, at times, closeness.

Before I came to this realization, I believed that how I operated in a relationship was normal, if not ideal. But by deepening my self-awareness and awakening to the programming of my internal operating system, I have learned that for much of my marriage, I have kept my wife at an emotional arm's length. And when she would approach me with healthy bids for affection or emotional expression, my operating system would commonly view those bids as signals of her neediness that encroached upon my independence.

Reflecting on this journey, can you sense that I used to think I was self-aware, but really wasn't? Before engaging with my therapist, I thought I knew myself, and I thought that how I operated was the ideal way to operate. The reality was that I did not have clarity on the self-protective motives, habits, scripts, and tendencies baked into my internal operating system. But by discovering that I do have an operating system and connecting with it more deeply, I not only deepened my self-awareness, but my path for vertical development became clear: I needed to upgrade my operating system to become less self-protective and dissociative and more value-creating and connected to my feelings.

My Wife Deepening Her Self-Awareness

Now let's look at my wife, Jena. As I engaged in efforts to awaken to my internal operating system, Jena gradually expressed more interest in awakening to her own. She engaged with my therapist and garnered similar awareness and insights to those I had. But a unique part of her journey was that, during the therapy process, she began learning about ADHD, and she began to suspect that perhaps she had a form of it. Upon getting tested, she learned at the age of 34 that she had a form called ADHD-Combined.

ADHD-Combined is a diagnosis that suggests that she exhibits both inattentive and hyperactive impulsive symptoms. Of the two, she connects more with the inattentive diagnosis.

ADHD-Inattentive differs from the stereotypical presentation of ADHD because people with ADHD-Inattentive generally are not hyperactive. Instead, people with ADHD-Inattentive struggle with a sluggish cognitive tempo that often includes mental fogginess, slow working memory, and reduced brain activity. Compared to people without ADHD, people with ADHD-Inattentive have difficulty with processing speed, attention regulation, listening, engaging in routine chores, and following sequencing events or detailed instructions.

ADHD-Inattentive is wildly underdiagnosed, particularly in adults. In fact, ADHD researcher Len Adler reports that only 10 to 25 percent of adults with ADHD are actually diagnosed and adequately treated. And women seem to struggle with ADHD-Inattentive more than men.

ADHD has been a part of my wife's internal operating system her whole life. It has been influencing her motives, habits, scripts, and tendencies. Yet it was only upon diagnosis that she became aware of the automatic and nonconscious role it had been playing in her life. Like with me, for most of her adult life we could count her as part of the 80-plus percent of people who think they are self-aware, but really aren't.

Getting diagnosed with ADHD has led Jena to have the same epiphany that I had after engaging with my trauma therapist. Before her diagnosis, she believed that how she was wired to operate was normal, and even ideal. But now she has come to a deeper recognition that the wiring associated with her internal operating system is less than ideal and something that can be refined and improved.

In fact, she is a great case study for the three-step process for becoming better. Her diagnosis helped with the first two steps: learning more about her Being Side and deepening her self-awareness. As she said:

> After being diagnosed and learning more about it, I felt like I suddenly understood myself. All the clichés applied. The light bulb went off in my head. Pieces of my life and personality started to fall into place and make sense. I could now better pinpoint how I am

programmed to interact with the world. I have come to see that my hyperactive side manifests in social settings where I can struggle with impulse control conversationally. I have a hard time listening and tend to jump in and interject my thoughts, which is really frustrating for me. My inattentive side manifests stronger because it's more my default setting. I really struggle to think through logistics and the finer details with anything, even with something as simple as making dinner. And I have a hard time mapping out anything in the future and default to "I'll deal with it when it gets here."

This awakening had some immediate transformative effects for her. She explained:

I immediately started to accept myself more and started having more compassion for myself. All the traits I possess that make me frustrated with myself now have a name and a reason. I don't think of myself as "lesser," or at least not as capable, anymore. I notice when an ADHD trait is popping up and try to course-correct by using learned life skills whereas before I just thought "this is me and I hate it" and would get angry with myself. It's still a learning curve and I'm still trying to learn how to compensate for my ADHD, but it is better than where I started. Learning I had ADHD made me feel like I was more in control and allowed me an opportunity to seek treatment.

The Power of Awareness

If we want to *become better*, it is essential to deepen our awareness of our internal operating system. The power of doing this and awakening to the quality, functioning, and sophistication of our operating system is that if we find that it isn't operating in the most ideal ways, we can do something about it.

For me, learning about trauma and recognizing its fingerprints on my internal operating system led me to engage in two years of trauma therapy, specifically focused on helping me heal from my past trauma and upgrading my operating system. Of all of the things I have done to help myself become better, there is nothing that has helped me more than this therapy. I truly feel like a much better person than who I used to be. I am more able to connect to my feelings and emotions, more regulated, more mindful, more balanced, and more willing to attune to others.

For my wife, with an increased understanding of the role ADHD was playing in her Being Side, she wanted to do something to upgrade her wiring. Of this she said:

> Once I got diagnosed with ADHD, I was relieved, like I wasn't completely to blame for all my poor traits, the ADHD was, but it also was hard knowing I had it. ADHD now felt like a thing living inside me that I just wanted to surgically remove like an unwanted tumor. I could see when it decided to manifest, and it was so frustrating. It felt like a war I was having internally, fighting over control for my brain, and I was constantly the loser. I very much wanted treatment.

After doing some research, and knowing about how our internal operating system is controlled by our body's nervous system, she identified neurofeedback therapy as a treatment she wanted to engage in.

Neurofeedback therapy is a type of therapeutic intervention that aims to help individuals regulate their brain functions. It involves exercises that allow an individual to consciously modify their brainwave patterns, something that is tracked via real-time monitoring of brainwave activity, usually through an electroencephalogram (EEG). The exercises can be adapted to address different brain dysfunctions, such as hyperactivity and impulse control.

Having completed neurofeedback therapy, my wife said the following about her experience:

Getting treatment for my ADHD was a huge step for me. It really has changed, or made manageable, so many of those traits I don't like about myself. Learning there were treatment options that didn't involve medicines with scary side effects was a huge relief. I really feel as if I have had a massive change in myself. I think my biggest change is that I am calmer. I don't feel like I have live wires exposed and going off internally anymore. I feel more independent, emotionally regulated, and overall, more mature. I don't get overwhelmed as easily. I feel more proactive instead of reactive to life. It's not that my ADHD magically disappeared and I'm cured of it. I still struggle in some areas and can see ADHD playing a role in my life. I am not quite as focused as I would like to be, I still have room for improvement while having conversations, and details still aren't my superpower, but I have seen improvement in all those areas and love the progress I am making.

Jena explained further:

I was a pretty happy-go-lucky person before but I really, truly can say I am a happier person post-treatment. Treatment has helped me grow in ways nothing else ever had. Not any self-help books, not therapy, not the life skills I have in place to compensate. All those things were and very much are helpful and important. They are necessary in helping me navigate life better, but ADHD treatment helped me surge forward and take control of my life.

My wife has transformationally *become better*. What enabled this to happen wasn't the Doing Side interventions that we so commonly look to. It was a Being Side intervention focused on upgrading her internal operating system.

As you will come to see in part 3 of this book, engaging in trauma therapy or working to address ADHD can transformationally help us to *become better*. But realize that these are advanced and deep *becoming better* practices. We generally do not start with them. I will be giving you suggestions for practices that range from starter-level to these advanced-level strategies.

As you get deeper into your *becoming better* journey, definitely keep yourself open to more of these advanced strategies. In some cultures, engaging in some of these practices carries the stigma that the person is "weak." Both my wife and I have felt such stigma in our own journeys, but as we stepped into our respective practices, we quickly realized that it is unfounded.

Key Discoveries

Thus far, I have given you a taste of how my wife and I went from thinking we were self-aware to truly deepening our self-awareness. We went from thinking we were navigating life in optimal ways to realizing we have limitations and self-protective wiring associated with our internal operating systems that were holding us back from being the people, parents, partners, and overall positive influences that we desired to be. I hope you get a sense of how impactful this deepened self-awareness has been for us.

I want you to experience this same deepening of your self-awareness. To get you started, in the upcoming chapters I will present two frameworks based on decades of research from different fields of psychology that are designed to help you more fully awaken to and measure the current quality and sophistication of your internal operating system. And to really make these frameworks come to life, I will be inviting you to take two personal assessments designed to help you more objectively do this work.

By learning about these frameworks and taking these assessments, you will be able to get in deeper touch with the current wiring of your internal operating system and gauge the altitude on your

I have learned through
my own experience that the
deeper you go inward, the
more you can become better.

———————————————

Being Side. In the process of doing so, you will likely learn, as I have, that you have wiring associated with your operating system that feels good, right, and even ideal, but is actually holding you back from being the person that you truly want to be.

Finding this self-protective wiring that holds us back is never fun, but it is life-changing. I have learned through my own experience that the deeper you go inward, the more you can *become better*.

Applications for Leadership

I have yet to meet a leader who does not think they are self-aware. But from my experience, very few have an understanding of and connection to their internal operating system.

In fact, there have been multiple times when I have been brought in to work with an organization's executive team, and the CEO opts out of taking my self-assessments or receiving 360-degree feedback. When this happens, my impression is that these are leaders who have very self-protective internal operating systems. And in each instance where this has happened, the CEO has largely been viewed by their executive team as being a poor leader. In fact, one of these CEOs was fired in the middle of my work with his executive team because of his poor leadership.

On the other side of the coin, the very best leaders I have worked with generally are very connected to their internal operating systems. They have done the deep work of surfacing their fears, insecurities, and inadequacies and rising above them.

Have you done that deep work? If not, how much of a priority is it for you to do it?

Ready or not, we'll start that deep introspective work in the next chapter.

7

What Adult Development Stage Do You Operate From?

Life is a gift, and it offers us the privilege, opportunity, and responsibility to give something back by becoming more.

TONY ROBBINS

THE FIRST POWERFUL FRAMEWORK for gauging our Being Side altitude and the quality and sophistication of our internal operating system comes from developmental psychology. Developmental psychology began as a field of study in the 1880s and is focused on understanding how and why humans grow, change, and adapt over their lifespan.

We can break this field down into two areas of focus: child development and adult development.

Across its 140-year history, developmental psychology has largely focused on child development. From this research, we have learned that critical physical, cognitive, and emotional growth takes place throughout childhood in rather predictable stages. And at each stage, children have different needs for experiences and care in order to develop the appropriate cognitive, social, emotional, movement, and language skills necessary for healthy development into adulthood.

The primary reason for this almost exclusive emphasis on child development is that it wasn't until the 1960s that some developmental psychologists abandoned the assumption that people stopped developing once they reached adulthood.

These few psychologists started to ask the questions: Can adults develop? And, if so, do they go through different developmental stages, similar to children?

What they found is fascinating.

These researchers found that, yes, adults can develop. And, yes, there are different adult developmental stages. In fact, there are three primary adult development stages, each representing different levels of maturity and sophistication related to how they navigate life.

But what the psychologists also found is that while adults *can* develop, most do not. Specifically, they have found that, across all adults, 64 percent do not develop beyond the first adult development stage, 35 percent develop to the second stage and stall out there, and only 1 percent develop to the third stage.

We have gained four valuable insights from this research.

First, there is a direct match between what I have been describing as the quality and sophistication of our internal operating system and these three levels of adult development. Adults at lower development stages have lower-quality internal operating systems wired more for self-protection than adults at higher stages, whose operating systems are wired more for value creation.

Second, in comparing childhood development to adult development, what developmental psychologists have found is that children develop rather automatically, which is essentially a function of their age. But when it comes to adult development, given that so few develop beyond the first stage, adults do not seem to develop as a function of age but rather as a function of effort. Thus, while all adults can upgrade their internal operating system, most do not put in the effort to do so.

My personal belief is that most people do not get beyond the first adult development stage, or get stalled at the second, because of a combination of not understanding these stages, not fully realizing that they have a Being Side, and not knowing how to go about upgrading their internal operating system. Hence why I am writing this book.

The third insight is that the only way to advance from one adult development stage to the next is by engaging in vertical development. While horizontal development may improve one's functionality through gaining knowledge, skills, and abilities, it is only vertical development that leads to the growth in maturity and sophistication of one's Being Side.

Fourth, by understanding the three adult development stages, we can better gauge the stage we are in and the corresponding quality of our internal operating system. We can also gain clarity about where we need to go next if we want to continue our *becoming better* journey.

So let's dive into the three stages of adult development.

The Three Stages of Adult Development

The primary way to distinguish between the three stages of adult development is to recognize that, at each stage, our internal operating system is wired to fulfill different needs. At the lower adult development levels, our needs will be more simplistic and self-protective, and as people progress from one level to another, their needs will become more refined and value-creating.

The labels I use for these three adult development levels are Mind 1.0, Mind 2.0, and Mind 3.0. I use "Mind" to signify that our mind is the home of our internal operating system. And I use the numbers

"1.0," "2.0," and "3.0" to signify that as we advance from one level to the next, there is an upgrade in our operating system.

Let's start by exploring the first stage of adult development, Mind 1.0.

Three Adult Development Levels

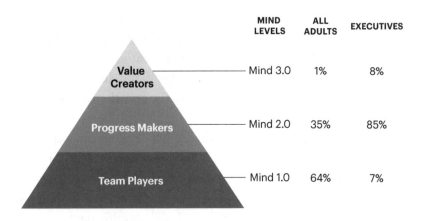

Mind Levels	All Adults	Executives
Mind 3.0	1%	8%
Mind 2.0	35%	85%
Mind 1.0	64%	7%

Value Creators — Mind 3.0
Progress Makers — Mind 2.0
Team Players — Mind 1.0

Mind 1.0: Team Player Mode

We have all been in Mind 1.0. So whether we are in Mind 1.0 now or have advanced beyond it, we should all be able to relate to it.

When someone operates primarily in Mind 1.0, their internal operating system is wired to fulfill the needs of safety, comfort, and fitting in. As a result, their nervous system is sensitive to and wants to avoid situations where they may be unsafe, uncomfortable, and not fit in. In fact, at this stage, being in these situations is among our biggest fears.

Because they are programmed in this way, one hallmark of Mind 1.0 people is that they are short-term-oriented and reactive as opposed to intentional and mindful. They take little thought for their future and are simply trying to survive the present. If they are feeling unsafe, uncomfortable, or like they aren't fitting in, their body reacts in a self-protective manner designed to alleviate these anxieties. As examples, Mind 1.0 people are prone to resist change and get defensive when receiving feedback. This is because change and feedback generally make Mind 1.0 people feel unsafe, uncomfortable, and like they may not fit in. And when they feel this way, they react in a manner that protects them in the moment, generally oblivious to how their self-protective reactions may negatively impact others or ultimately limit them.

Another hallmark of Mind 1.0 people is that they seek to join social groups that will help them feel safe, comfortable, and like they belong. These groups can be one's family, friend groups, organizations, religions, or other communities. When Mind 1.0 people join these groups, they don't step into them and try to take charge. They give up their power and independence to the leaders of the group in exchange for the hope that the group will help them feel comfortable. They essentially say, "I'll let the group, or the leaders of the group, instruct me on how to think and operate, and I will gladly follow along, provided that the group also keeps me feeling safe, comfortable, and like I fit in."

These two hallmarks culminate in a third hallmark of Mind 1.0 people: Because they are prone to allow their circumstances or other people to dictate their direction and thinking, they generally operate as dependent thinkers. Of course, if we ask Mind 1.0 people if they are a dependent or independent thinker, they will say independent. But while they may think they are a self-directed being, they are generally not in touch with their internal operating system and how it is directing the majority of their thinking, feeling, judging, and acting to serve their self-protective needs of safety, comfort, and fitting in.

Brené Brown used to operate at a Mind 1.0 level when she instinctively avoided stillness and vulnerability. Stillness and vulnerability

By understanding the
three adult development
stages, we can better gauge
the stage we are in and the
corresponding quality of our
internal operating system.

———————————————

made her feel unsafe and uncomfortable, and if she was vulnerable, her internal operating system was wired to believe that she would be rejected or not fit in. Thus, while she likely perceived that she was self-directed, her operating system predisposed her to operate in a self-protective manner that kept her safe in the moment, but held her back from wholehearted living in the long run.

Also, remember Sheryl, my coaching client who had a lot of letters following her name in her email signature and kept getting passed up for promotion because she struggled to take initiative. She operated in Mind 1.0. For her, taking initiative felt unsafe and uncomfortable, and she feared that if it did not go well, she wouldn't fit in at her organization.

In Mind 1.0, people generally operate like a team player. They are wired to keep the peace, play nice, follow the rules, stay in their comfort zone, promote clear structure, and maintain order, while also avoiding being wrong, having problems, standing out, engaging in conflict, overextending, and failing.

Given that almost all adults get to the Mind 1.0 development level and 64 percent of adults operate there, you should be able to recognize this programming in your current or past self. Now, if you are currently at this level, there is nothing inherently wrong or bad about this. You just need to understand that at Mind 1.0 you possess programming for self-protection, which surely helps you feel more secure but is also likely holding you back from having the positive impact on your world that you aspire to have.

Mind 2.0: Progress Maker Mode

As one advances to the next adult development level, Mind 2.0, their internal operating system becomes wired to fulfill dramatically different needs. Specifically, Mind 2.0 people are wired to stand out, advance, and get ahead.

This is a transformational shift in how their body's internal operating system defines pain and pleasure. At the Mind 2.0 level, people are now willing to be unsafe, uncomfortable, and not fit in so that they can stand out, advance, and get ahead. This is a complete and dramatic rewiring. And when someone has made this shift, it is a signal that they have transformationally *become better*.

As people go from Mind 1.0 to Mind 2.0, they shift from being dependent thinkers to being independent thinkers. They start to develop their own ideas and strategies, and they become increasingly willing to push against the ideas, beliefs, and norms of their social groups. They are willing to do this because they no longer rely on their social groups to fulfill their needs. When they were in Mind 1.0, they avoided taking charge, but now they *want* to do so. They have their own ideas, beliefs, and perspectives that they think are optimal, and they want to employ them in a manner that allows them to better stand out and get ahead. Thus, Mind 2.0 people generally want to be leaders within their social groups. In fact, while research on the general public has found that 35 percent of people operate with a Mind 2.0 internal operating system, research on leaders has found that only 7 percent of leaders operate at the Mind 1.0 level and 85 percent operate at Mind 2.0.

At the Mind 2.0 level, being concerned about standing out, advancing, and getting ahead, people come across as progress makers. They are focused on getting things done, competing, hitting their numbers, being the expert, looking good, being right, being perfect, being efficient, and winning. They are very driven people, but their drive is generally targeted toward standing out, particularly in the short term. Thus they tend to be results- or outcome-focused. They are prone to lock in on clearing the next hurdle or the next benchmark, and they want to make sure they do it before others or in a better way than others. They also tend to care more about the accomplishment of outcomes than they do the people around them. In Mind 2.0, leaders may demand too much of their employees, parents may care more about crossing things off their to-do list than engaging with their children, and people may be willing to push others under the bus to get where they want to go. As a result, people in Mind 2.0 commonly come across as possessing lower levels of emotional intelligence.

As I reflect on my life through the perspective of these adult development stages, I can clearly see that from the age of 18 to about 34, I operated in Mind 1.0. In fact, I believe it was my strong Mind 1.0 mentality that steered me toward being a professor as opposed to a consultant, because it was a job with inherent safety because of its tenure system. But around the age of 33, I had the itch to do some consulting, so I took a leave of absence from my university and took a job at Gallup. If you recall, about a year into that role I was fired. In hindsight, I recognize that I was probably operating too much as a Mind 1.0 dependent thinker and not enough as a Mind 2.0 independent thinker.

Getting fired rocked my world. At the time, I felt blindsided, but I can now see that this experience was pivotal in jarring me out of my Mind 1.0 development stage. Upon landing back at my university and doing some work on myself, I upgraded my internal operating system. I can now recognize this shift because I let go of the need to play it safe and became driven to advance myself, improve my financial status, and stand out, even if that meant doing things that pushed me out of my comfort zone. For example, one of the ways I felt like I could stand out was by writing a book. So I wrote *Success Mindsets*, and even the word "Success" can have a Mind 2.0 connotation to it. And I was willing to go into debt to invest in my book so that I could get accolades like "*Wall Street Journal* and USA *Today* best-selling author." I was driven, goal-oriented, and outcome-focused.

Given that 85 percent of leaders operate primarily in Mind 2.0, most of the people I work with and coach operate at this level. They emphasize results over culture. They are more concerned about the short term than the long term. They are reluctant to try new ways of operating and hold on to what has worked in the past because they want to feel certain that they can hit their short-term objectives. While this is justifiable, it is also self-protective, it limits their agility, and it holds them back from creating value in the long term.

While there are limitations to operating at a Mind 2.0 level, it is a step up from Mind 1.0 in the adult development journey. Getting to Mind 2.0 does require a refinement and upgrade of one's internal operating system. In Mind 1.0, people are self-protective dependent thinkers. They have a narrow window of tolerance for safety, comfort, and fitting in. While this keeps them safe and comfortable, it is a rather simplistic way of operating. In Mind 2.0, while they are still rather self-focused, their thinking is not as self-protective or dependent. They have widened their window of tolerance for feeling unsafe, uncomfortable, and like they don't fit in, which allows them to operate at a higher, more sophisticated level: as results-focused, independent thinkers.

Mind 3.0: Value Creator Mode

For someone to advance to the third level, Mind 3.0, they must again upgrade their internal operating system, which involves reprogramming themselves to fulfill dramatically different needs from Mind 1.0 and Mind 2.0. Specifically, Mind 3.0 people become wired to contribute, add value, and lift others.

This is another significant shift in how their body's internal operating system defines pain and pleasure. They are no longer wired to fit in (Mind 1.0) or stand out (Mind 2.0). In fact, they are now willing to be unsafe, uncomfortable, and put themselves on the back burner to fulfill the Mind 3.0 needs of contributing, adding value, and lifting others.

As people make the shift from Mind 2.0 to Mind 3.0, there are three major changes that occur.

First, they become interdependent and complex thinkers. They come to recognize that their Mind 2.0 independent ideas and strategies weren't the only or best ones to have. They realize that taking in various and diverse perspectives advances their ability to think and operate at increasingly effective levels. Also, not being concerned about standing out in the short term, they can focus on a longer time horizon. Together, these shifts create the mental and emotional space for them to engage in more strategic and complex thinking, planning, and decision-making.

Second, they become less self-focused and more other-focused. In Mind 1.0, they are focused on *their* safety, comfort, and fitting in. In Mind 2.0, they are focused on *their* standing out, advancing, and getting ahead. In Mind 3.0, they are focused less on themselves and more on their impact. In fact, a key distinguishing aspect of most Mind 3.0 people is that they have a clear and inspirational purpose for their life that involves contributing to something bigger than themselves. They want to create value and are wired to do so.

Third, they dramatically elevate their level of self-leadership. People in Mind 3.0 have developed a mature, sophisticated, and regulated nervous system with even wider windows of tolerance associated with safety, comfort, standing out, and getting ahead. Their body's nervous system is so regulated that they are balanced and under cognitive and emotional control when these needs are threatened or they experience significant stress, uncertainty, or complexity. With higher regulatory abilities, people in Mind 3.0 possess a great capacity to continually create value in alignment with their purpose, despite the difficulties, challenges, or setbacks that may occur.

Altogether, people at Mind 3.0 are very elevated on their Being Side. They have the capacity to be and stay mindful, balanced, and centered; engage in courageous vulnerability; stand up to power; challenge conventional wisdom; let go of what has served them in the past; explore beyond the conventional; and elevate others. As a whole, they operate not as team players or progress makers, but as value creators.

Unfortunately, research has found that only 1 percent of the public and 8 percent of executives operate at this level. Thus, there is a good chance that most of us have never spent much time associating with someone at Mind 3.0. A common comment I get from the people I coach is: "I am not sure I have a close role model at the Mind 3.0 level, someone to look to, pattern myself after, or learn from. I have primarily been following and patterning myself after Mind 2.0 leaders and people."

But when we do meet Mind 3.0 people, they are generally creating a massive amount of value for others. In fact, whenever we study the lives of great people and leaders—people like Martin Luther King, Jr., Nelson Mandela, Harriet Tubman, Michelle Obama, Jacinda Ardern, and Abraham Lincoln—we do not find perfect people, but we do find complex, interdependent thinkers who possess refined nervous systems that allow them to stay balanced under pressure and continually focused on contributing to a clear and inspirational purpose that is bigger than themselves. In fact, each of these people has been willing to put themselves in harm's way and not personally advance in order to fulfill their bigger purpose.

In my studies of leaders and people, I believe I have identified a variety of people who seem to operate at this Mind 3.0 level. I do think that Brené Brown has become one of them. To me, she seems genuinely focused on creating value for others by helping people live wholeheartedly. She also seems to have refined her body's nervous system to the degree that she is willing to put off her self-protective needs and has developed the courage to step into the messiness and discomfort of stillness, vulnerability, and empathy.

Another example is Satya Nadella, the CEO of Microsoft. Some of the signals of him operating at the Mind 3.0 level include:

- His primary focus as CEO is on culture. In fact, he says that the "C" in CEO stands for "Curator of Culture." His focus is not on results or outcomes in the short term but on creating the conditions that allow for positive and growing results in the long term.

- When he became CEO, one of his biggest priorities was coming up with a new mission statement. He knew the company needed a clear, inspirational, and stakeholder-centric purpose that would encourage employees to take their eyes off of themselves and put them on something bigger than themselves. The mission statement that was created is: "To empower every individual and every organization on the planet to achieve more," which is focused on creating value for others.

- When problems have occurred in the organization, Nadella has stayed balanced and centered. For example, in 2016, Microsoft researchers unveiled an artificial intelligence–based chatbot called Tay. Upon releasing Tay to the public, Twitter trolls discovered that if they sent Tay racist, sexist, and other hateful messaging, the bot would regurgitate it publicly. It was a public relations nightmare for Microsoft. Despite the setback, Nadella did not come down hard on the project's leaders. Instead, he sent them a message that said, "Keep pushing, and know that I am with you."

The Value of Understanding the Three Adult Development Levels

There are two massive benefits to understanding the three adult development levels.

The first is that it helps us deepen our self-awareness and connection to the quality and sophistication of our internal operating system. It gets us more in touch with our Being Side. For me, it does so in a few different ways.

Knowing the adult development levels has allowed me to ask and attempt to answer a couple of questions that few people ever ask, which are: What is my Being Side altitude? Or, stated differently,

What is the quality of my internal operating system? Without having this framework, it would be difficult for me to identify the quality of my Being Side, and I would have little reference for knowing whether I had a low or high Being Side altitude.

Understanding the adult development levels has also allowed me to more clearly see and more deeply appreciate the significant role our internal operating system plays in our motives, thinking, tendencies, actions, and overall, how we approach and navigate life. And, to be honest, while the framework is helpful for personal introspection, I find it easier to use it to gauge the Being Side altitude of others. When I work with leaders or a coaching client, I can quickly home in on what adult development level they are operating from. But for myself, I recognize that I have some self-protective biases that make me reluctant to see or fully appreciate some of my Mind 1.0 or Mind 2.0 tendencies.

In fact, one of the biggest challenges we face on our *becoming better* journey is coming to terms with the idea that our Mind 1.0 or Mind 2.0 wiring, while it feels natural and right, is not ideal and ultimately limits us.

I experienced this when I started working on my vertical development with my therapist. In the course of working with her, I routinely said things along the lines of: "Why would I do that if it feels so uncomfortable or wrong to me?" Then, she would explain to me that while avoiding connection may feel right and comfortable, it was ultimately limiting and was causing me to behave in a manner that was negatively affecting my relationships and connections with those around me. Upon hearing things like this, my mind would immediately turn to the adult development levels, and I would be forced to see how my internal operating system was operating at a Mind 1.0 or Mind 2.0 level, which leads me to the second massive benefit of understanding the three adult development levels.

The second benefit is that once we gain greater clarity about our current altitude and quality of being, the framework allows us to more clearly see where we need to go to *become better*. If I am in Mind 1.0, I might be a lot like Brené Brown prior to her personal transformation, consistently avoiding stillness and vulnerability as a form of self-protection. If so, it is a signal that I am going to have to work on letting go of my self-protective needs for safety, comfort, and fitting in, and work on refining my internal operating system to be more focused on being intentional, taking initiative, and being more purpose-oriented so that I live more wholeheartedly. Stated differently, I am going to have to work on widening my window of tolerance associated with my self-protective needs.

If I am in Mind 2.0, I might find a certain degree of success because of my ability to think independently, take initiative, and be driven to accomplish my goals or generate certain outcomes. But just because I am successful at hitting targets does not mean that I have "arrived" or that there isn't room for becoming better. If I want to *become better* as a Mind 2.0 person, I am likely going to have to work on becoming more purpose-focused, more concerned about the process of getting the outcomes as opposed to the outcomes themselves, and more concerned about creating value for the people around me than creating value for myself. Stated differently, I am going to have to work on widening my window of tolerance associated with not hitting short-term targets or milestones while I simultaneously become more focused on creating long-term value.

The adult development levels framework should help you better identify where you are at and where you need to go to *become better*. But to help us further, let's add some nuance to our understanding of this framework so that we can introspect with even greater precision.

Center of Gravity

To be fair, the notion of these adult development stages is not cut-and-dried. If you are anything like me, I imagine that you can see all three levels in yourself. I have come to learn that we do have a dominant and default adult development stage that we operate from, but that doesn't mean that we can't temporarily operate with motives, thinking, and actions typical of a different development stage.

Thus, another helpful way to think about these stages is to consider our center of gravity, or the default stage that we tend to operate from. For example, that stage might be Mind 1.0, where we spend approximately 60 percent of our time. But we might also spend about 25 percent of our time operating with Mind 2.0 tendencies, and 15 percent with Mind 3.0 tendencies.

Our Center of Gravity

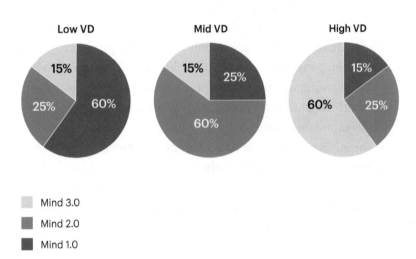

Low VD — 15% / 25% / 60%

Mid VD — 15% / 25% / 60%

High VD — 15% / 25% / 60%

Mind 3.0
Mind 2.0
Mind 1.0

When I first learned about the adult development stages, my immediate thought was: "I think I am a Mind 3.0 person." I immediately brought to mind a bunch of examples from my life of the times when I operated with the motive and focus to create value for others. But what I didn't fully appreciate at the time was that while there had been instances where I operated at Mind 3.0, I really spent the vast majority of my time at Mind 2.0. It wasn't until later, when I had learned more about the adult development levels and given myself time and space to introspect more accurately, that I came to realize that my center of gravity was Mind 2.0.

Understanding this notion of "center of gravity" allows us to ask another set of powerful questions that should help us awaken to the altitude of our Being Side and the quality and sophistication of our internal operating system. These questions are:

- What is my center of gravity?

- What is the percentage of my time that I seem to be spending at each of the different adult development stages?

- What stage do I seem to default to under times of stress, pressure, or complexity?

Additionally, looking at the quality of our internal operating system through the "center of gravity" lens gives us another way to think about how we go about elevating our Being Side. We can now ask and take action on this question: How do I go about spending a greater percentage of my time in Mind 3.0?

Vertical Development Assessment

If you would like to receive more objective information related to the quality and sophistication of your Being Side, and identify your center of gravity, I have developed a free Vertical Development Assessment: https://ryangottfredson.com/vertical-development-assessment.

The assessment and its results are designed to help you in your process of awakening to the current state of your internal operating system. It has 15 questions and should take you less than 10 minutes to complete.

The results that you receive will identify your center of gravity, where you seem to primarily operate from. The results do not mean that you spend 100 percent of your time at that particular level, but it is likely the most dominant level that you operate from and the default level that you fall into when you face pressure, stress, or complexity.

Key Discoveries

In this chapter, I have leaned on adult development theory to present one framework for deepening your self-awareness and getting in touch with the quality and sophistication of your internal operating system. I hope you have found it eye-opening.

What mind level do you usually operate from: Mind 1.0, Mind 2.0, or Mind 3.0? What needs is your internal operating system most programmed to fulfill? And which best represents your center of gravity?

In the coming chapters, we'll cover a related and richer framework to further help you connect with the current quality of your Being Side.

Applications for Leadership

In my experience working with leaders and leadership teams, I have observed that most leaders operate with a Mind 2.0 internal operating system. They are primarily focused on getting short-term results and generally lead through hierarchical control. This commonly shows up in a tendency to micromanage and being consumed with fighting fires.

One of the first steps I take with them is to help them awaken to how operating in this way may lead to some short-term benefits but is not a strategy for scaling up and long-term success.

Once the leaders get the vision of higher-level leadership, I try to help them upgrade their internal operating systems to the Mind 3.0 level by helping them establish a Mind 3.0 foundation to lead from. Specifically, I show them how to

- develop a clear, inspirational, and stakeholder-centric purpose statement that helps them focus on creating value over the long term

- establish a strong and healthy accountability culture that allows them to lead through empowerment as opposed to control

- create a climate where their employees focus less on their self-protective needs and more on creating value for their stakeholders and customers.

8

What Is the Quality of Your Mindsets?

Nobody likes to be driven by someone else; it feels like being pushed. But when someone can show us how to be bigger on the inside—in our attitude and mindset— that can help attract or pull us toward what we can become.

MARK SANDBORN

REMEMBER, A CORE ASPECT of our internal operating system involves how we make meaning of our world. Thus, another way to investigate the quality of our operating system is to investigate the quality of our meaning-making.

The best way to do this is to inspect our mindsets. If we can get in touch with our mindsets, and the degree to which they are wired for self-protection versus value creation, that will allow us to more fully awaken to the quality and sophistication of our internal operating system and the altitude of our Being Side.

I am sure you hear the word "mindsets" all the time. It is generally used to refer to our attitude toward something. For example, I have heard of "entrepreneurial mindset," "abundance mindset," "leader mindset," and "creative mindset." But the true nature of our mindsets is much deeper than simply our attitude toward something. Our mindsets are actually specific types of neural connections in our brain that play three pivotal jobs in the translation of signals from our senses and our ultimate response to those signals.

The Three Jobs of Our Mindsets

The first job of our mindsets occurs at the gate to our brain, where our nervous system sends information from our senses. At the gate, our mindsets' first job is to be a filter and determine whether the signals being sent to the brain are things that should be ignored or let into our brain for further processing. If our mindsets are more wired for self-protection, they will be more sensitive to signals of potential danger and more prone to filter those into our brain for further processing than if they are more wired for value creation.

The second job of our mindsets is to assign meaning to the signals that are filtered in. Given that we receive so many signals from our senses, manually interpreting all of them is laborious, so our nervous system develops patterns of interpretation. This interpretive role of our mindsets is their most well-known job. It helps explain why two different people can encounter the same situation, let's say receiving constructive criticism, and one person takes it as an attack, while the other interprets it as something that might help them learn and grow.

Our mindsets' third job, then, is to activate our brain's and body's response to the signals taken in (job #1) and how they are interpreted (job #2). For example, let's compare Jasmine and Andrew, whose different mindsets cause them to see and interpret feedback differently. At separate times, Jasmine and Andrew both receive feedback that their communication during a meeting was off-topic and derailed the conversation. For both of them, their mindsets filtered this information in for further processing. Since Jasmine's mindsets are more self-protective, her brain automatically interpreted this feedback as an attack. As soon as that happened, Jasmine's nervous system activated a defense mode that led her to dismiss and ignore the feedback. Andrew has more value-creating mindsets, which led to his brain automatically interpreting this feedback as potentially beneficial for his learning and growth. With this interpretation, Andrew's nervous system created cognitive and emotional space to absorb the feedback, allowing him to process adjustments that he could make moving forward to become a greater value creator in similar situations.

Our mindsets are an integral aspect of our body's internal operating system. Our body uses our mindsets to be more efficient in how we process our world. Yet, while the programming associated with our mindsets is surely efficient, that does not necessarily mean it is effective. Mindsets can vary in terms of their sophistication, or the degree to which they are wired for self-protection or value creation.

I want to introduce you to a framework that spans four different sets of mindsets as a way to help you evaluate the quality of your internal operating system. Having worked with thousands of people to help them awaken to the quality of their mindsets, and having had to awaken to my own mindsets, I've learned that this awakening is not easy. In fact, when people have self-protective mindsets, invitations to investigate their mindsets are generally met with resistance, if not all-out rejection. So, before we dive into the framework, I want to cover a couple of ideas to prepare you for exploring the quality of your mindsets. First, I'll be up-front about why connecting with our mindsets is not easy. And second, I'll invite you to take my Personal Mindset Assessment so that you'll have some more objective data and results related to the current quality of your operating system and elevation along your Being Side.

Once we put labels and descriptions to our mindsets, we become empowered to deepen our self-awareness, explore the quality of our mindsets, and determine altitude on our Being Side.

———————————————

Why It Is Difficult to Get in Touch with Our Mindsets

Let me ask you a question: Do you believe that how you currently think is the best way you know how to think?

Of course you do. If you felt you could think better and knew how to think better, you probably would.

One of the primary reasons most people do not inspect and get in touch with their mindsets is because our mindsets and their related thinking—whether high- or low-quality—feels right and natural to us. When my wife sees a clown and gets scared, this feels right and natural to her, even if it may not be a helpful or effective response. When pre-transformed Brené Brown was asked what she does when she can't fix something she would like to fix, rather than get vulnerable and admit her struggles or ask for help, she said she would "clean the house. Eat peanut butter. Blame people. Make everything around me perfect. Control whatever I can—whatever's not nailed down." Maybe you can relate! This self-protective operation felt right and natural to Brené until she started to question whether her thinking was, in fact, the best way to think.

For almost my entire adult life, I felt like I navigated relationships in an effective way until I realized my marriage was not what I wanted it to be, started working with a therapist, and discovered that I have a more avoidant attachment style that tends to hold others at a distance. I had believed that my thinking about how to engage in relationships was the best way to think because keeping people at a distance felt so natural and right to me.

A second reason most people do not inspect their mindsets is because our mindsets do most of their work below the level of our consciousness. They are performing their three jobs—filtering information in, interpreting it, and setting up our body's response—automatically and efficiently. We simply don't even know they are there and doing these jobs.

A third reason most people are not in touch with their mindsets is because they don't know what mindsets are out there and their various intricacies. Without having labels and descriptions for mindsets, it is nearly impossible to even attempt to get in touch with them. But with these labels and descriptions, we become empowered to deepen our self-awareness, explore the quality of our mindsets, and determine the altitude on our Being Side. Hence our upcoming mindset framework.

Personal Mindset Assessment

Before we get into that framework, I invite you to take my free Personal Mindset Assessment. Taking this assessment before we dive into the specific mindsets is intended to keep you as unbiased as possible for this evaluation.

But there are a couple of things I want you to know about this assessment before taking it. First, it focuses on four different sets of mindsets that have received over 30 years of attention. The items included in the survey are based on validated research instruments that have been used over this time span. Second, each mindset set represents a continuum ranging in quality and sophistication. The assessment is designed to help you identify where along that continuum your mindsets currently reside.

The assessment is 20 questions and will take roughly 7 minutes to complete. It is designed to compare your responses to those of the over 50,000 people who have taken it, allowing me to provide you with an individualized report that identifies the relative quality of your mindsets. The individualized report you will receive will identify the current quality of your mindsets along each of the four mindset continuums.

Please complete the assessment here: https://ryangottfredson .com/personal-mindset-assessment.

Having used this assessment with hundreds of groups and thousands of people and sifted through the data, I have learned and observed some interesting things.

First, I have found that only 2.5 percent of people who have completed the assessment are in the top quartile for all four sets of mindsets. What this tells me is that almost all of us have some self-protective tendencies built into our internal operating systems. This should not surprise us, particularly given that (1) most people have never given concerted effort to work on and improve their mindsets, and (2) adult development research has found that 64 percent of people operate in Mind 1.0, where there is strong wiring for self-protection.

Second, I have learned that it's common for people to get upset or even angry about their results. I understand why this is. It is because our mindsets lie at the core of our being, and if we get results that we don't love, we are getting an indication that our being is *off* in some way. That is not easy to sit with. I commonly see this manifested in two ways.

The first way occurs when one receives results that differ from how they identify or see themselves. Unfortunately, this puts people in a tough spot. This conflict between one's results and identity ultimately suggests that either the assessment is wrong or they lack a bit of self-awareness. I am definitely not going to say that the assessment is 100 percent accurate (it is impossible to assess something that we are largely not conscious of with perfect accuracy). But I also know that, as we previously discussed, research has revealed that 80 percent of people think they are self-aware but actually are not.

The second way people get upset or angry about their results is that they feel so justified and right about their current self-protective mindsets. If people have self-protective mindsets, they have them for a reason. The mindsets keep them safe and protected from something they believe could cause them harm. But when one is locked into ensuring their own safety and protection, it's difficult to explore seeing the world in a different way. For example, one mindset set deals with how people view risk. If someone gets results that suggest that they tend to avoid risks, they wonder, "How is this bad? Aren't risks dangerous and shouldn't they be avoided?" What they are revealing is their window of tolerance for risk. They are aware of the short-term negative effects that can occur by taking risks, but they likely haven't come to fully see and appreciate the long-term limitations of their "risk is bad" mindset.

In fact, when I first learned about the quality of my mindsets, which were originally very self-protective, I was in absolute denial. I believed that my thinking was the best way to think. I felt justified in my self-protective mindsets, and I hadn't yet been exposed to their long-term limitations. At the time, I couldn't comprehend what it would be like to see and interpret my world in different ways. But once I pieced together the framework I am about to describe, it helped me to see the limitations of my mindsets, and what better ones might be. Learning about these mindsets helped me *become better* by allowing me to get in touch with my internal operating system. I hope this framework has a similar effect on you.

If you haven't yet taken the Personal Mindset Assessment, you can do that now at ryangottfredson.com/personal-mindset-assessment.

The Mindset Framework

When I first learned what mindsets were—that we all have them, and that they play a foundational role in our lives—I became thirsty to learn more about them. I wanted to learn what different types of mindsets were out there, and which types I had.

Being a professor and researcher, I decided to dive into the vast body of academic work on the topic and try to identify any mindset that has been researched. What I found was four sets of mindsets that have been studied for over 30 years, each stemming from research within different fields of study: social psychology, educational psychology, marketing, and management.

I also learned that these different sets of mindsets are unique and distinct from each other because they each revolve around different self-protective fears and value-creating tendencies. Across each set's continuum, there is one mindset that contains self-protective programming and another that has value-creating programming. And what 30-plus years of mindset research has discovered is conclusive: Mindsets on the self-protective side of the continuum may have some short-term self-protective benefits, but they are ultimately limiting in the long term; whereas the more value-creating mindsets are associated with a wider window of tolerance for the fears connected to the self-protective mindsets, and ultimately lead to much more positive long-term benefits.

Having identified these four sets of unique mindsets, I compiled them into one framework (see the image below), which to my knowledge represents the most comprehensive and research-backed mindset framework ever compiled. This is not to say there are no other mindsets beyond these four groups. I believe there are others, but these are the only 4 with over 30 years of research backing.

Self-Protective	Value Creating
Fixed	Growth
Closed	Open
Prevention	Promotion
Inward	Outward

We are next going to walk through each of these four sets of mindsets. And, to avoid making this an insanely long book chapter, I am breaking it into several different chapters. The upcoming four chapters each focus on one of the four sets of mindsets. To make these mindsets come to life for you and help you better introspect about the quality of your own mindsets, I will open each chapter with a situation where there is a choice about how to navigate forward, present a core tension that is at the heart of that choice, and then demonstrate how people with the value-creating mindset are programmed to operate differently than those with a self-protective one.

Key Discoveries

At this point, we are barely scratching the surface of our mindset content. But hopefully you have a greater appreciation of the following ideas:

- Because our mindsets are central to our body's internal operating system and how we process and interpret information, they are a great aspect to evaluate to determine our Being Side altitude.

- Introspecting about our mindsets can be difficult because (1) we don't have labels or descriptions that allow for self-evaluation, and (2) they are a core part of who we are, so if we get signals or results that indicate that we don't have high-quality mindsets, we might get defensive.

- You will be invited to consider the quality of your mindsets across four different mindset sets, with each set representing a continuum of mindset quality that ranges from self-protective to value-creating. The primary question you will want to get answers for is: Where does the quality of my mindsets fall along each continuum?

Applications for Leadership

I have been fortunate to work with thousands of leaders, ranging from mid-level managers all the way up to CEOs, and have observed something interesting: The higher the leader is in the organizational hierarchy, the less prone they are to introspect about their mindsets, ruminate about where their mindsets have come from and how they are holding them back, and actually put in concerted effort to elevate them.

In fact, I have worked with numerous executive teams where the CEO has expected their team to take mindset development seriously, but opted out of my offer to help them with their own mindsets.

Unfortunately, this trend runs opposite to what I think is ideal. Ideally, we would have the highest-level leaders set the example of focusing on and elevating their mindsets. But I also recognize that higher-level leaders generally have more demands on their time and attention than lower-level leaders, and they may assume that they need less work on their mindsets, both of which can be hurdles to personal and leadership development.

However, there are two profound benefits for the leaders who invest in awakening to and improving their mindsets. First, these leaders develop a greater capacity to juggle their responsibilities and demands effectively. This is because they spend less time being self-protective and more time being empowering. Second, these leaders enhance their leverage on their organization. They establish a culture and process that costs little to them, but pays off in massive returns in greater engagement. Either way, leaders who do deliberate work on their mindsets operate at a higher, more sophisticated level that is generally experienced by the organization as being transformational.

So, as we dive into the mindset framework, consider: How seriously are you going to apply this content to your life and leadership?

9

Fixed and Growth Mindsets

Ever since I was a child, I have had this instinctive urge for expansion and growth. To me, the function and duty of a quality human being is the sincere and honest development of one's potential.

BRUCE LEE

COACH MY son's basketball team, which is made up of 10-year-olds. As a coach, I want to help my players develop skills that will set them up for success as they get into junior high and high school. One vital skill that I want my players to learn is the ability to shoot a layup (close-range shot) with their nondominant or off hand. This ability makes them a much more dynamic and effective player, and it would be highly unlikely for a player to make a junior high or high school basketball team without excelling at this move.

Knowing this, I ask my players to try shooting layups with their off hand during practices and games. For my young players, this is no easy request. Let me explain why.

The request to shoot with one's off hand creates a tension between short-term and long-term benefits and consequences that my players have to navigate. And it is their fixed and growth mindsets that dictate their body's automatic response to my request.

In fact, I get three different responses when I ask my players to shoot layups with their off hand.

The first response is that they do not even attempt it.

Why do you think this is? Why do some players resist my instruction?

From what I have experienced as a basketball player and observed as a coach, there are three potentially negative consequences to attempting to shoot a layup with one's off hand:

1   They will feel awkward and uncomfortable.
2   They will look bad and uncoordinated.
3   They will likely miss the shot.

So, for the players who don't attempt it, what I am observing is their internal operating system caring more about avoiding these negative consequences in the short term than the long-term benefits of developing this skill.

The second response is that they are willing to try to shoot with their off hand in practice, but not in games.

Why is this?

Well, understandably, there's more pressure to feel good, look good, and make their shots during games, where their family and friends are watching and maybe even filming them from the stands. Plus, they want to win, and they do not want to let their team down. This added pressure of a game setting causes them to be more self-protective than they are in practice.

While I understand this pressure, something I have learned but they don't fully grasp is that when players attempt a new skill during a game, their growth and development *dramatically* accelerates.

The third response is rare, but I do have one or two players who are willing to try to shoot a layup with their off hand in practice *and* in games.

Why are they able to do this when their peers resist it?

Ultimately, it is because they have a mindset that is wired more for long-term value creation. They have a wider window of tolerance for feeling bad, looking bad, and missing their shots. Their mindsets and body are okay with these potentially negative consequences in the short term, because they recognize that developing skills and becoming the player they desire to be in the long term requires wading into feeling bad, looking bad, and making mistakes. For them, they see and value the longer-term time horizon more than any potential discomfort in the moment.

Recognizing these three different types of responses, consider this question: Do you think they are rationally thought out, or more instinctual and automatic?

My experience is that they are instinctual and automatic. Their responses are a byproduct of the mindsets that are core to their body's internal operating system. And, across these responses, do you sense a continuum of mindsets that range from being wired for short-term self-protection to long-term value creation?

The tension that my players are experiencing in this example is between looking good in the short term and learning, growing, and developing in the long term. And it is the quality of our mindsets along the fixed-to-growth mindset continuum that directs us to operate in one direction or the other, or somewhere in the middle.

Let's now dive into each mindset. In doing so, I am going to paint the edges of the continuum by explaining how people with stronger fixed and growth mindsets tend to operate. But please recognize that the quality of our mindsets can rest anywhere along the continuum. Your mindset assessment is designed to help you roughly identify where along this continuum your current programming resides. Also recognize that multiple books have been written just on fixed and growth mindsets. We are only spending one chapter on this topic. So, if you want greater depth on this mindset set, I recommend Carol Dweck's book *Mindset* or my book *Success Mindsets*.

Fixed Mindset

People with a fixed mindset carry the implicit belief that we cannot change our talents, abilities, and intelligence. They tend to think, "I am who I am, and there isn't anything I can do about that."

When people possess this belief, they do not want to fail or look bad because, without the belief that they can improve their talents, abilities, and intelligence, they tend to interpret failing as a sign that *they* are a failure.

Thus, people with a fixed mindset have internal programming that often makes them operate in a manner that ensures they look good in the short term. This is just like my basketball players whose internal operating systems resisted trying a layup with their off hand.

There are six aspects of this mindset that are crucial to point out.

First, a fixed mindset is justifiable and surely feels right to those who have one. I mean, who likes to fail or look bad? No one, really. When my fixed-mindset basketball players refuse to try a layup with their off hand and use their dominant hand to make the layup, they will generally puff up their chest a bit and may give me a smug look, as if to say, "See? Why should I shoot with my off hand when I can be awesome right now!"

Second, a fixed mindset is self-protective. With a fixed mindset, our body's natural programming will continually direct us toward protecting our image in the short term.

Third, a fixed mindset generally operates below the level of our consciousness. When my players refuse to shoot with their off hand, I don't think they do any sort of mental calculation before making the decision, such as thinking through the pros and cons of their options. I think they simply follow their internal operating system's self-protective programming.

Fourth, a fixed mindset means having a narrow window of tolerance for failure and looking bad. Because of this narrow window of tolerance, we see common patterns of operation from those with a fixed mindset. The most common pattern is to avoid learning zone challenges, challenges that push them out of their comfort zone. This is because learning zone challenges put them at risk for failure and looking bad in the process of rising above the challenge. Other operating patterns include seeking approval and validation from others, resisting feedback, not putting forth effort to develop, comparing themselves to others, and giving up easily. For example, have you ever played a board game with someone who got to the point where they knew they were going to lose, so they toppled the table? They simply could not tolerate losing, partly because their fixed mindset was interpreting that situation as: If I lose, that means that I am a loser.

Fifth, a fixed mindset is not very cognitively and emotionally sophisticated. Rather, it is evidence that we have instinctual and reactive self-protective tendencies. When faced with a learning zone challenge, people with a fixed mindset allow themselves to be driven away from it because of their fear of failure, and they have a hard time connecting to the long-term benefits of taking it on. This was me in my freshman year of college. I wanted to be a doctor, so I signed up for the pre-med program, which required me to take an advanced chemistry class. I did not do very well in the class. I got a C grade. To me, this was a failing grade and a sign that I was not cut out to be a medical doctor. So, after that class, I dropped out of the pre-med program and switched my major. This was largely an instinctual reaction. I did not take much time to think and recognize that the path from freshman in college to medical doctor would be fraught with significant challenges that I would have to work through and overcome. Thus, rather than stepping into the challenge, I was wired to avoid it.

Sixth, because of all these reasons, a fixed mindset is evidence that our Being Side altitude is not very high. If we want to *become better*, we are going to have to widen our window of tolerance for failure and looking bad, which will allow us to be more willing to take on and work through learning zone challenges.

Carol Dweck, the pioneer of fixed and growth mindset research, has reported that roughly half the population has more of a fixed mindset, and the other half more of a growth mindset. I find similarly in my research. In fact, I find that the group that struggles the most with a fixed mindset is business leaders and executives. I believe this is because they feel so much pressure to always look good.

One of the common ways I see leaders' fixed mindsets manifest is that they are reluctant to innovate. When I ask them why, they generally identify the same fears and concerns that my young basketball players have when they are asked to shoot a layup with their off hand. They tell me how it is uncomfortable; there is no guarantee of success, particularly in the short term; and it may prevent them from hitting their expected numbers and looking good during their next evaluation cycle. That all makes sense. It is justifiable. But if an organization continually avoids innovating, it is unlikely they will be able to grow and create value in the long run. As a result, fixed-mindset leaders tend to stifle their organization's long-term viability.

Unfortunately, what people with a fixed mindset generally fail to recognize is that their focus on avoiding looking bad or failing ultimately dooms them to look bad and fail in the long term. This is because their reluctance to step into challenges and put forth effort to get better ultimately limits their rate of growth and development, and their peers who have more of a growth mindset and develop at a faster rate will ultimately outperform them.

Growth Mindset

People with a growth mindset carry the implicit belief that we *can* change our talents, abilities, and intelligence. People with this belief do not see failure as a sign that they personally are a failure, but as a great opportunity to learn and grow. They are less concerned about looking good in the short term and more interested in developing for the long term.

Unlike those with a fixed mindset, people with a growth mindset are willing to attempt new skills and take on big challenges, like shooting with their off hand or innovating, despite the fact that they may not be successful on their first attempt, all-out fail, or look bad in the process. They are willing to do this because (1) they do not believe that a lack of success when trying something new or taking on a big challenge says anything about who they are and their worth, and (2) they inherently recognize that developing new skills and taking on big challenges helps them learn and grow, which will allow them to be more effective, successful, and a greater value creator in the future.

There are six aspects of this mindset that are crucial to point out.

First, a growth mindset is not self-protective. It is value-creating. People with a growth mindset are less concerned about protecting their image than they are about how much they learn, grow, and improve their ability to contribute in bigger and better ways in the future.

Second, people with a growth mindset have a wide window of tolerance for failure and looking bad. Their body's nervous system is not hypervigilant to how they are perceived by others, and they can withstand the emotional discomfort of trying something outside of their comfort zone.

Third, our growth mindset generally operates below the level of our consciousness. When faced with a challenge, those with a growth mindset generally react immediately with expressions like, "Bring it on!", "I've got this!", or "No challenge too big."

This is demonstrated well in a research study conducted by Carol Dweck and her colleagues. The researchers had individuals take a mindset assessment to distinguish who had more of a fixed mindset

People with a growth mindset are less concerned about looking good in the short term, and more interested in developing for the long term.

_____

or more of a growth mindset. Then they had all of the participants engage in an exam that had eight easy questions and four really challenging ones that were above their level of knowledge and skill.

What the researchers were doing was setting up these people to fail, and they wanted to gauge whether they would respond differently to failure depending on their mindsets. What they found was that those with a fixed mindset were really pleased with themselves during the eight easy questions, but as soon as they hit the four challenging questions, their thoughts quickly deteriorated. They started to talk negatively to themselves, they reduced their effort to work through the problems, and they changed the subject from the test to talking about their past successes. But those with a growth mindset responded very differently. When they hit the four challenging questions, instead of beating themselves up they started encouraging themselves, they stayed focused on working on the problems, and they engaged more deeply with the four difficult questions.

Do you think the participants' responses were conscious, thought-out responses or mindset-driven, automatic reactions? They were likely mindset-driven, automatic reactions representing how they are wired to navigate in challenging performance situations.

Fourth, a growth mindset is very cognitively and emotionally sophisticated. As I have articulated, people with a growth mindset are more willing to experience emotional discomfort in the short term in exchange for a future benefit. This means they are more comfortable when approaching and engaging with learning zone challenges. It is a demonstration of a significant amount of mental maturity, which leads to the fifth aspect.

Fifth, because of all these reasons, a growth mindset is evidence that the altitude of one's Being Side is high. It can be observed that those with a growth mindset are primarily disposed to operating in value-creation mode and staying there, despite pressure to look good or not fail in the short term.

Sixth, all people learn and grow. So the fact that you have learned and grown is not necessarily an indication that you have a growth mindset. A growth mindset is revealed in performance contexts when there is pressure to look good because something is on the line, like a game setting for my basketball players.

Key Discoveries

In summary, our internal operating system currently has programming for navigating the tension and pressure between looking good and learning and growing. If our operating system steers us toward looking good in performance contexts, that suggests that we have more of a fixed mindset. But if our operating system directs us toward learning and growing, we likely have more of a growth mindset.

Applications for Leadership

If you were to ask a room full of leaders if any of them had a fixed mindset, do you think anyone would raise their hand? I don't.

Yet, despite the fact that most leaders believe they have a growth mindset, I have discovered that over 60 percent of leaders have a fixed mindset. It is the mindset that leaders most commonly struggle with.

As I mentioned, I think one big reason leaders struggle with it so much is because they are in a position where there is a lot of pressure to look good. But the very best leaders have developed a wide window of tolerance for looking bad. This allows them to more readily make decisions with long-term, value-creating implications as opposed to short-term, self-protecting implications.

10

Closed and Open Mindsets

If someone is able to show me that what I think or do is not right, I will happily change, for I seek the truth, by which no one was ever truly harmed. It is the person who continues in his self-deception and ignorance who is harmed.

MARCUS AURELIUS

AM GOING TO DESCRIBE a scene from a movie, and I'm curious if you would respond in the same way as the focal character if you were in the same situation. This scene comes from the movie *Pitch Perfect*, which is about a female collegiate a cappella group trying to make it to the national collegiate a cappella finals.

I want you to put yourselves in the shoes of Aubrey, the group's leader. Aubrey is a senior in college and also the most senior member of the group, which is largely made up of freshmen and first-timers, people who do not have near the experience or expertise that she does. Aubrey has proven herself successful in the past, having guided the previous year's team to the national finals.

As Aubrey, you desperately want to get back to the finals and win this time around. If you could do that, it would be life-changing. But if you do not make it to the finals, you feel it will be a stain on your resume. While the pressure is high, you are confident. You feel like you have a proven formula for success. You got the team to the finals last year, and you believe you can do it again with this new group.

During rehearsals one day, things aren't clicking the way you know they need to. Despite all of your hard work, your teammates aren't performing at a very high level, and you are starting to question whether they have what it takes. Your group also seems to sense that something is off, and your co-captain, Chloe, comes forward and admits that she isn't performing up to par because of issues she has been having with her vocal cords. You suggest that maybe someone else needs to take her part.

Chloe suggests that Beca should take her part. But Beca is the one person in the group that you do not have a lot of confidence in.

Just as your frustration at this suggestion starts to rise within you, Beca snarkily says, "I would be happy to do it if I got to pick a new song and do the arrangement."

You interpret this comment as an inexperienced group member questioning your strategy for success, which is based on years of experience. You are a little put off.

At that moment, Beca steps forward to push the issue. She says that your choice of song is tired, old, and not as dynamic as it needs to be. She recommends that you take two songs from different genres and mash them together to create something more fun and dynamic.

You feel like you are losing control of the situation.

I want you to think about how you would respond to this recommendation to drop the song you selected and go in a different direction.

To help you weigh your options, let's consider a couple of aspects of what might be going on within you. First, consider your window of tolerance. Where do you think you would be on your window of tolerance? Would you be in the middle and unfazed? Would you be close to the edge, frustrated, and about to lose it? Or would you already be over the edge?

Second, what is the likelihood that you are going to seriously consider the suggestion to scrap the current song you are working on and go with Beca's idea of taking two songs and mashing them together?

Whether you realize it or not, there is a tension that exists in this situation. On one side of the tension is the option to move in the direction of certainty and control by sticking with what you know, what you believe to be your proven formula for success. On the other side is the option to reconsider if your song choice is really the best option for obtaining your goal of winning the national championship. It is an option that implicitly involves you admitting that you made a less-than-optimal decision to begin with and that your "proven formula" has limitations.

Now, do you think the quality of your window of tolerance might impact how you navigate this tension? Undoubtedly! The further you are from the center of your window of tolerance is likely going to dictate how self-protective you are in that situation.

How Aubrey responded in the movie was by very sharply saying, "Okay, let me explain something to you because you still don't seem to get it. Our goal is to get back to the finals and these songs will get us there. So, excuse me if I don't take advice from some alt-girl with her mad-lib beats because she has never been in a competition. Have I made myself clear?!"

Clearly Aubrey fell more on the side of self-protection, choosing to go with what she felt was right as opposed to seeking the truth about her song choice and what might be most optimal for the group. While this stance helped her feel more stable and secure in the short term, it limited her team because the song that she had chosen was stale, and blending songs from two different genres was actually a great idea, albeit one that made her feel uncomfortable.

When our body is programmed to lean toward holding on to what we believe to be right as a way to protect our ego and identity, we have more of a closed mindset. But when we lean toward questioning our beliefs and perspectives in an attempt to find truth and think optimally, regardless of our ego or identity, we have more of an open mindset.

Let's dive into each of these mindsets.

Closed Mindset

People with a closed mindset have a strong sense that what they know is right, and they have internal programming that makes them prone to take the course that is most likely to uphold this belief. They possess self-protective wiring that is designed to prevent them from finding themselves in a position where they have to admit they are wrong or others will see them as being wrong. They fear that if they are wrong, or seen as wrong, others will lose respect in them.

Just as with a fixed mindset, there are six aspects of a closed mindset that are crucial to point out.

First, a closed mindset is justifiable and surely feels right to those who have one. I mean, who likes to admit they are wrong or have others see them as being wrong? No one, really. Putting ourselves back in Aubrey's shoes, there are many reasons we could justify our self-protectiveness:

- We do have experience.

- We have been successful in the past with this strategy.

- The recommendation for change does not come forward in a very effective way.

- The recommendation comes from someone with little experience.

- Trying out this new idea might cause division in the group.

- The recommendation is something that falls outside of our area of expertise.

We might wonder, how are we supposed to lead a group if we aren't an expert in what we are leading?

While the reasons to resist the recommendation are numerous and justifiable, if you have seen *Pitch Perfect* you would know that this idea of doing mashups from different genres is a great idea, one that they adopt, and it not just gets them to the national finals but helps set them apart and win the competition.

Second, a closed mindset is self-protective. Aubrey's defensive response was designed to protect her, her path, her identity as a leader, and her certainty about her strategy. While she could claim her defensiveness was for the group's sake, she ultimately wasn't doing what was best for the group. She was doing what was best for her, which was protecting herself from having to admit her "proven formula" was not optimal.

Third, a closed mindset generally operates below the level of our consciousness. Let's be honest, Aubrey was put on the spot. It was not an easy position to navigate. She did not have the time to logically think through the pros and cons of the various responses she could have provided. She ran with what her internal operating system's programming directed her to do. It was instinctual and subconscious.

Fourth, a closed mindset is an indication of a narrow window of tolerance for being wrong or seen by others as wrong. Because of this narrow window of tolerance, there are common patterns of operation from those with a closed mindset. They tend to position themselves where they are "in charge," to be the one providing answers (as opposed to asking questions), and to avoid feedback and new perspectives. And they tend to see disagreement as a threat and get defensive. As a result of all this, they also tend to be narrow-minded and out of touch with reality.

Fifth, a closed mindset is not very cognitively or emotionally sophisticated. The reality is that a closed mindset is evidence that we have instinctual and reactive self-protective tendencies that protect us in the moment but hold us back from thinking and operating in elevated ways that are most optimal for our future. Specifically, when our knowledge, expertise, or authority is called into question, our closed-mindset programming causes us to respond in a manner that protects us from the fear of losing our standing as an expert or authority in that moment, even if the new ideas coming forward may set us on a better trajectory for future success.

We see this all the time with feedback. How do many people respond to feedback? They get defensive. Why do they get defensive? Because their closed-mindset programming is set up to protect them in the moment. Their defensiveness allows them to hold on to the belief that they or their manner of operation is right. But if we dismiss feedback that could help us *become better*, we just stunted ourselves and our future.

Sixth, because of all these reasons, a closed mindset is evidence that the altitude on our Being Side is not very high. If we want to *become better*, we are going to have to widen our window of tolerance for being wrong or having others see us as wrong. If we can do that, we will be able to do a better job of being less concerned about being right and more concerned about finding truth and thinking optimally.

Unfortunately, what people with a closed mindset generally fail to recognize is that, unless they are 100 percent holding on to truth, their focus on being right will ultimately doom them to be wrong. For example, in the 1500s, the Catholic Church held the geocentric belief that the sun revolves around the earth. I suppose this supported their view of our centrality in the universe. So, when Galileo Galilei proposed that the Earth revolves around the sun, the Catholic Church had him put under house arrest rather than exploring the veracity of this idea. In this instance, the church was protecting itself from being seen as wrong, but this ultimately doomed them to *be* wrong.

Open Mindset

People with an open mindset have internal programming that leads them to find truth and think optimally, even if that means having to let go of what they think is right. There are five aspects of this mindset that are crucial to point out.

First, an open mindset is not self-protective. It is value-creating. While people with a closed mindset generally believe they are right, people with an open mindset believe that even though they may know a lot, it is possible for them to be wrong. They want to get as close to the truth as they can, even if that means admitting their thinking was off or wrong. They know that the closer they are to truth and the more optimally they think, the more they will be able to create value.

Second, people with an open mindset have a wide window of tolerance for being wrong or viewed as wrong. To them, being wrong is a sign of growth. They recognize that if they are proved wrong, they have learned something and are now better off. As a result, people with an open mindset do not identify strongly with any particular beliefs. So, when they have to let go of a belief, they aren't losing part of their identity, they are elevating their perspective and thinking. Thus, people with an open mindset create psychological space to be wrong when they or their thinking is called into question, they are able to stay calm, balanced, and centered, helping to ensure they learn, make sound decisions, and adapt appropriately.

Third, an open mindset generally operates below the level of our consciousness. Consider the times we receive feedback. As I mentioned, people with a closed mindset have a nervous system that quickly responds to feedback by getting defensive. This is a result of their narrow window of tolerance. But people with an open mindset have a nervous system that does not rush in to self-protect. With their wider window of tolerance, their nervous system stays calm, allowing them to create space for the feedback and explore it.

People with an open mindset
have internal programming that leads
them to find truth and think optimally,
even if that means having to let go
of what they think is right.

———————————————

Fourth, an open mindset is very cognitively and emotionally sophisticated. As I have articulated, people with an open mindset are more willing to experience the emotional discomfort of being wrong or seen as wrong in exchange for a future benefit: getting closer to truth and thinking more optimally. This allows them to create space for alternative ideas and perspectives and let go of any ideas or beliefs that are suboptimal. Plus, I think you would agree that someone who can admit they are wrong demonstrates a significant amount of cognitive and emotional sophistication.

Fifth, for all of these reasons, an open mindset is evidence that the altitude on our Being Side is high. It is an indication that we are primarily disposed to operating in value-creation mode and staying there, despite pressure to be right or to maintain the appearance of being right in the short term.

Key Discoveries

In summary, our internal operating system has programming related to how we navigate the tension and pressure between being right and thinking optimally. If our operating system steers us toward protecting our need to feel right over thinking optimally in performance situations, that suggests that we have more of a closed mindset. But if it directs us toward thinking optimally instead of being right in those situations, that suggests that we have more of an open mindset.

Applications for Leadership

Across the struggling executive teams I have worked with, I have observed a theme: Individual members hold the belief that they are not part of the problem or the reason why the organization isn't operating at a higher level. The executive team members are quick to point the finger at others in the organization or contextual factors for any problems or low-quality leadership. They are closed to the idea that they could be part of the problem.

Of course, this is a self-protection mechanism. Their body holds the belief that if they admit they haven't been operating at a high level or have misstepped, they are putting their job and career on the line. This is justifiable. But it is also something that will prevent the team and the organization from turning their difficult situation around.

From my experience, an executive team will not be able to elevate their organization until they become willing to fully see the role they have played in it not operating at a higher level. This acknowledgement seems to be a prerequisite for change and improvement. But it is scary, and it takes a lot of cognitive and emotional sophistication.

Further, I have observed that when leaders take ownership of their missteps, acknowledge their role in any dysfunctions, and demonstrate a commitment to becoming better, they become more respected by the people they lead, not less.

11

Prevention and Promotion Mindsets

You were put on this earth to achieve your greatest self,
to live out your purpose, and to do it courageously.

STEVE MARABOLI

O FEEL INTO THE TENSION associated with prevention and promotion mindsets, let's step into a sailing analogy. Let's imagine a ship captain who is out at sea, traveling along just as we are traveling through life. One day a big storm comes on the horizon directly in front of the ship. This storm creates a tension for the ship captain, forcing them to decide how to best proceed. The tension is between staying safe and secure or making progress toward an intended destination. Certainly, the captain could change course by going back the other way or going to a harbor to wait out the storm. But they could also take precautions and prepare the ship for taking on the storm, which would allow them to continue to make progress toward the destination.

The way our internal operating system is programmed to lean amidst this tension is revealing of whether we have a prevention or promotion mindset. When someone has a prevention mindset, they are programmed to be more focused on staying safe, protected, and problem-free. With a promotion mindset, they are programmed to be more focused on their intended destination, which should ideally be a purpose focused on creating value for others.

Let me give you a couple of situations where I have seen these mindsets come up for myself and others.

I am a professor at California State University, Fullerton. It is a regional university that is largely a commuter school. This means that of the roughly 40,000 students, less than 10,000 live on or around campus, and most commute in. Additionally, Cal State Fullerton largely serves a demographic that comes from more challenging financial backgrounds. Because of this, I have a number of students who are non-traditional college students, meaning they are in their late 20s or older. Whenever I have a non-traditional student, I am always curious about their story and ask them to share it if I get the chance and they seem open to it. One of the common stories that I hear from them is simply, "I wanted to go to college when I was younger, but I didn't have the money, and I was scared to take out a loan." Not always, but commonly, they will express regret at not getting a loan and attending college earlier in life. For these students, they encountered a storm while at sea. They had a choice: play it safe by not getting a loan and figuratively going to a harbor until the storm passed, or prepare to take on the storm, get a loan, and begin their college journey and career sooner.

Another place I have seen and personally felt the dynamics of prevention and promotion is in parenting. Over the years, at times, my children have asked to go play in the rain, play in mud, or do something with a little bit of risk involved, like try skateboarding. In these moments, I feel the tension that I have described. If I let them do these things, I will likely have a mess to clean up or they might get hurt, both things that I don't want. But I also want them to enjoy life, explore, have fun, play, and be a kid. Thus, I am torn: Do I pull the reins back on my children to ensure my comfort and ease my anxiety? Or do I fulfill one of my purposes as a parent, which is to help them experience a full and rich life, and let them engage in these activities?

Within you is programming that regulates how you approach life. Do you think you are more wired for safety and comfort or for purpose and goal achievement? Let's dive into prevention and promotion mindsets to better answer this question.

Prevention Mindset

People with a prevention mindset are risk- and problem-avoidant. As a ship captain, their primary goal is to not sink. Thus they see risks and problems as threatening to their survival and usually avoid them. They have fears and anxieties of bad or uncomfortable things happening, and their focus is more on avoiding these things than on accomplishing a goal or fulfilling a purpose.

Similar to fixed and closed mindsets, there are six aspects of a prevention mindset that are crucial to point out.

First, a prevention mindset is justifiable and surely feels right to those who have one. I mean, who likes to have problems, have things go squirrelly, and be uncomfortable? No one, really.

For most of my adult life, I have operated with a prevention mindset. As I have mentioned, one of the ways this manifested for me is that I never wanted to be an entrepreneur. This stance felt justifiable because not only did being an entrepreneur seem risky and full of discomfort, but I could point to my father's struggles as an entrepreneur. I didn't want to find myself in the same position.

Second, as you have probably already sensed, a prevention mindset is self-protective. Not getting a loan to go to college, not letting my kids play in the rain, and not being an entrepreneur surely protected me in the moment. But these are all things that can hold us back and stunt our growth or impact over the long term. Thus, as with fixed and closed mindsets, a prevention mindset seems to provide us with some self-protective benefits in the short term, but limit us in the long term.

Third, our prevention mindset generally operates below the level of our consciousness. When I made my decision to go get a doctoral degree, it felt very conscious and rational. I did put a lot of time and effort researching my different options and coming up with a career path that I thought was best for me. But what I didn't realize then that I realize now is that I had a prevention mindset undergirding all of my thinking and decision-making. As I was weighing my options, one of the main things that I was looking for, because of my prevention mindset, was the likely stability of my future. I now see that one of the main reasons I chose academia instead of a corporate or entrepreneurial route is that it felt safer to me because of the tenure system and the general stability of the educational system. My prevention mindset was playing a significant role in my decision-making without my awareness.

Fourth, a prevention mindset is an indication that we have a narrow window of tolerance for risk, having problems, and experiencing discomfort. For people with a prevention mindset, it is easy for them to become anxious, unsettled, and overly protective. Let me give you an example.

One of my past coaching clients was Tom, a vice president in a medium-sized technology organization. For the first part of his adult life, Tom was in the military, where he saw significant combat experience. Upon leaving the military, he was an emergency medical technician (EMT), administering first aid to people who had experienced horrific accidents.

My coaching process with Tom began after I had taught him and his peers about the mindset framework I am walking you through.

So, when I met with him for our first coaching call, I asked him if the mindset material made sense to him. His response was, "Yes, except for the prevention and promotion mindsets." He went on to explain that his life in the military and as an EMT had taught him that problems should be avoided at all costs. At the time, I validated his perspective and explained that I had a vertical development exercise we would do that would allow us to better feel into and discuss his concerns. Through that exercise, what we learned was that as a leader, his primary focus was not on fulfilling a purpose or accomplishing goals but on not having any problems pop up that day or that week. He wasn't very willing to take initiative, he steered away from risk, and he struggled to delegate because he didn't trust others to fulfill the tasks handed to him without problems occurring.

In fact, during one coaching call he said to me, "In my line of work, when problems occur, people can die." This comment shocked me, and it also seemed to reveal his window of tolerance for problems. After gathering myself and slowing his racing nervous system down, I calmly asked him: "In your current line of work within your technology company, is there anyone that is facing a life-or-death situation?" He acknowledged that no one was. This question allowed me the opportunity to help him see that his time in the military and as an EMT caused his nervous system to be constantly on guard for problems in truly life-or-death situations, and while that functionality likely served him well in those roles, it was holding him back as a leader in his technology company. If he was going to be successful as a leader in the company, he couldn't keep treating potential problems as being life-threatening.

Unfortunately, Tom came to this realization too late. Shortly after this conversation, he was asked to retire early because his overprotectiveness fueled by his prevention mindset was negatively impacting the people he was leading and limiting how much value he was creating for the organization.

The fifth important aspect of the prevention mindset is that it is not very cognitively and emotionally sophisticated. Just as with fixed and closed mindsets, a prevention mindset is evidence that we have instinctual and reactive self-protective tendencies that protect us in the moment but hold us back in the future. College-age people who don't go to college because of a fear of taking out a loan commonly place a ceiling on their long-term career that, down the road, they will wish was higher. Parents who don't let their children play in the rain may cause their children to be sheltered and overly precautious themselves. My dad's self-protective fears surely wore off on me. My decisions to be a professor and avoid being an entrepreneur put a cap on my income-making abilities. And for my coaching client, while he did not have many work-related fires rise up within his division, he was not seen as a high-potential leader and was ultimately asked to leave.

Sixth, because of all these reasons, a prevention mindset is evidence that the altitude on our Being Side is not very high. If we want to *become better*, we are going to have to widen our window of tolerance for risk, problems, and discomfort. If we can do that, our focus will move away from short-term self-protection to long-term value creation.

Promotion Mindset

People with a promotion mindset possess an internal operating system that is wired for purpose fulfillment and goal accomplishment. There are five aspects of this mindset that are vital to understand.

First, a promotion mindset is not self-protective. It is value-creating. While people with a prevention mindset want to prevent bad or uncomfortable things from happening, people with a promotion mindset want to make great things happen. In fact, what I have discovered is that people with a promotion mindset have two things that those with a prevention mindset generally do not. First, they have a clear destination that they are shooting toward. Normally, this is a destination on the horizon, a place they have not reached yet but one that is meaningful for them to get to. Second, they have a clear purpose for getting there. The more that purpose is connected to creating value for others or something bigger than themselves, the better. Further, I have discovered that if people do not have a clear destination to aim at, they will default to a prevention mindset.

Second, people with a promotion mindset have a wide window of tolerance for problems and risk. When people with a prevention mindset experience or anticipate problems or risk, they get anxious. People with a promotion mindset cognitively and emotionally understand that to get from where they are now to their intended destination, a place they have not yet been to, they are going to encounter problems and risk. They recognize that problems and risk are a necessary part of the journey, and thus they create space for them. While they may try to prevent problems from occurring, that is not their primary focus. And when they do experience challenges, they do not get sent to the outer edges of their window of tolerance. They are able to stay balanced and centered and choose to view those problems as a signal that they are making progress toward their destination and fulfilling their purpose.

Third, a promotion mindset generally operates below the level of our consciousness. When people have a prevention mindset, their body's nervous system is hypervigilant to what might go wrong. They automatically and nonconsciously take a precautious approach to life. But when people have a promotion mindset, their body's nervous system is automatically and nonconsciously focused on what might go right, particularly as it relates to them getting closer to their destination and fulfilling their purpose. Stated differently, people with a promotion mindset have a bias favoring courage and value

People with a promotion mindset have a bias favoring courage and value creation, whereas people with a prevention mindset have a bias that favors difficulty avoidance and self-protection.

———————————

creation, whereas people with a prevention mindset have a bias that favors difficulty avoidance and self-protection.

Fourth, a promotion mindset is very cognitively and emotionally sophisticated. Whenever I teach groups about the difference between prevention and promotion mindsets, I will inevitably have a prevention-minded person raise their hand and ask, "But some risks should be avoided, so where do we draw the line?" I love this question, and I am prepared for it. To answer it I show the group an image of a hiker at the bottom of a mountain looking up toward the summit, and I explain the following.

Having a promotion mindset does not mean that we don't care about problems and risks. It means we are, first and foremost, focused on getting to the top of that mountain. But we also want to get up there in the safest and most problem-free way possible. Someone with a promotion mindset who wants to climb the mountain does not just roll out of bed in the morning and start walking. They set their destination and then do everything in their power to mitigate any foreseeable problems and risks that might arise along their journey. They make sure they have necessary clothes and equipment, are well supplied with the food and water they will need, and check the weather to ensure the conditions are right. Having a promotion mindset is more cognitively and emotionally sophisticated than prevention because it allows us to simultaneously take into consideration our destination and purpose along with known problems and risks. Someone with a prevention mindset only takes the problems and risks into consideration, and thus never really has a reason to climb a mountain, something that is inherently risky and has a likelihood of problems occurring.

The fifth important aspect of a promotion mindset is that, for all these reasons, it is evidence that the altitude on our Being Side is high. It is an indication that we are primarily disposed to operate in value-creation mode and stay in it despite pressure to avoid problems or prevent bad things from happening. From my study of people with prevention and promotion mindsets, I have come to believe it is only possible to live with courage if we have a promotion mindset.

Key Discoveries

In summary, our internal operating system currently has programming related to how we navigate the tension and pressure between avoiding problems and reaching a destination. If our operating system cares more about avoiding problems in performance situations, that suggests that we have more of a prevention mindset. But if its focus is more about reaching a destination, that suggests a promotion mindset.

Applications for Leadership

As I have worked with leaders who operate from different vertical development levels, I have observed that depending on their level, they take on a different mindset along this prevention-to-promotion continuum.

- Leaders at Mind 1.0 take on a prevention mindset, where they prioritize comfort over results and purpose.

- Leaders at Mind 2.0 take on a results-focused promotion mindset, where they prioritize short-term results over comfort and purpose.

- Leaders at Mind 3.0 take on a purpose-focused promotion mindset, where they prioritize the fulfillment of a meaningful purpose over comfort and short-term results.

Knowing this, if I am working with a new organization or executive team, one of the first questions that I ask their leaders is: "How do you measure success?" Their answer to this is generally quite revealing of the mind level that the organizational leaders operate from. If they operate at Mind 1.0, they generally answer by saying something along the lines of, "We want to have a family-friendly place for our employees to work." If they operate at Mind 2.0, they typically refer to numbers and outcomes, something along the lines of, "Double-digit growth year-over-year." But if they operate at Mind 3.0, they often recite their purpose statement and describe how they are creating value for their customers.

So, if I were to ask you how your organization measures success, how would you answer?

Chapter 12

Inward and Outward Mindsets

---

*In every moment . . . we choose to see others either as people like
ourselves or as objects. They either count like we do or they don't.*

THE ARBINGER INSTITUTE

A S WE NAVIGATE LIFE, we are inevitably intersecting with others.
At any intersection, we bring along certain needs we have that
we'll call "me needs," and the other parties bring their own, and
we'll call these "they needs." The tension that exists at these
intersections is: Do we seek to fulfill our "me needs" or help others fulfill their "they needs?" Of course, if the "me needs" and the
"they needs" are aligned, we may not feel any tension. But if they are
misaligned, we will feel some tension. And, the greater the misalign-
ment, the greater the tension we will feel.

The degree to which we have an inward or outward mindset dictates whether we are wired more to fulfill our "me needs" or more
to help others meet their "they needs." People with an inward mindset are more strongly programmed to fulfill their "me needs," while

people with an outward mindset are more strongly programmed to get in touch with others' "they needs" and help satisfy them.

To get into this, let's consider a variety of common intersection points, step into the common "me needs" and "they needs" at these intersections, and explore the different ways we can navigate these situations.

Imagine being caught in traffic while driving in the far right lane on a freeway. You look in your rearview mirror and see a car speeding toward you on the shoulder of the freeway. They come up past you and put their blinker on, wanting to get into your lane just in front of you. In this moment, what would you be thinking and feeling, and how would you respond?

In this situation, you have some "me needs" that likely include getting to your destination in a timely manner, having traffic move in a fair and organized way, and being seen and respected by those around you. But a tricky aspect of this situation is that you do not necessarily know what all the "they needs" are of this person who sped past dozens of cars on the shoulder and now wants into your lane right in front of you. Clearly, one need is to get into your lane, and that may be all—or there could be a need to get the woman in the back seat to a hospital because she is in active labor. We will not know, and we will likely never know. So, in this context, to what degree are you focused on fulfilling your "me needs" of fairness, being respected by others, and getting where you need to go in time, and to what degree are you creating space for their "they needs," whatever they may be? Your thoughts about the driver of the other car and your next actions will likely be revealing of the degree to which you have an inward or outward mindset.

Next, let's explore a team setting. Every semester I assign my students to work in teams of five for a group project. On the day that they are assigned teams, they are rather anxious. This is because they are uncertain about whether this new group of people they will have to work with will be respectful of and help them accomplish their "me needs." Additionally, they recognize that across the group, each student may have different "me needs" that could include getting a good grade on the project, being treated in a respectful manner, working well together, or having to do as little work as possible.

Put yourself in my students' shoes. If you have just been assigned to a new team to work with for the next three months and are feeling anxious, when you meet your group for the first time, do you think your mind and body are going to be more focused on ensuring your "me needs" get met or on getting to know, understand, and fulfill your new team members' "they needs?"

What I have found across my college classes is that over 60 percent of my students have inward mindsets. This means that for a group of five, on average at least three of the group members are approaching the group wondering, "How is my team going to help me accomplish my 'me needs'?" And two or fewer of the members are approaching the group focused more on understanding their teammates' "they needs," establishing a cohesive "we need," and then working toward fulfilling all of these needs. What I have learned is that multiple people focused primarily on their own "me needs" is not a good recipe for success on group projects.

Working in teams is something that I have personally struggled with. Earlier in the book, I referenced how when I played basketball growing up, I struggled to be a team player. This is because I was more programmed to fulfill my "me needs" of scoring and racking up great statistics than I was about my team members' "they needs" and my team's collective "we needs."

Consider teachers guiding workshops or teaching in an educational setting, athletic setting, at church, or at an organization. As someone who has extensive experience being a student as well as teaching in all of these settings, I know that the tension between "me needs" and "they needs" always exists for teachers. What I have observed is that teachers with an inward mindset seem to be more preoccupied with their "me needs," which shows up in them seeming to be more focused on impressing their audience, having their experience be easy and comfortable, sticking to their script, and getting through their material than they are about connecting with their audience. Throughout my teaching career, it has been easy for me to recognize how I have misstepped in all of these ways more times than I would like to admit. I have also observed that teachers with an outward mindset, those focused on seeking to understand, connect with, and address the "they needs" of their audience, are not only willing to engage in more difficult but effective activities, embrace the discomfort of vulnerability, and put their script on pause, but they are also the most effective teachers.

The reality is that our intersections with others are almost infinite, and we possess programming that makes us more wired to lean toward fulfilling our "me needs" or toward connecting with and fulfilling others' "they needs." And while our programming may not be a big deal when it comes to any single interaction, we continually have so many interactions that even a slight difference in our programming along this inward-to-outward mindset continuum would make a huge difference in how we navigate life and interact with others across our lifespan. For example, even a shift from 51/49, inward/outward, to 49/51 can have a meaningful impact.

Let's now step more deeply into each of these mindsets.

Inward Mindset

As mentioned, people with an inward mindset are programmed to be more focused on "me needs" than "they needs" in social situations. The general result of this programming is that those with an inward mindset are prone to see themselves as being more important than others, which causes them to tend to see others as objects and treat them as such.

From my experience, there are two primary explanations for why people develop inward mindset programming. First, when people are raised in situations where their "me needs" are not valued or taken care of by their caregivers, their body becomes wired to be more inward-minded as a way to ensure that their "me needs" get met. Second, they operate in a culture that socially or formally incentivizes individual performance, often through competition. In these settings, individuals become programmed to care more about "me needs" than "they needs," which could be those of their customers, coworkers, or business partners. For example, have you ever had the experience of buying something, like a car, house, or security system, and you felt like the sales rep saw you more as a dollar sign than as a person? That would be an indication that they have more of an inward mindset.

Similar to fixed, closed, and prevention mindsets, there are six aspects of an inward mindset that are crucial to point out.

First, and this might be obvious, but being wired to fulfill our "me needs" is justifiable and surely feels right to those who have an inward mindset. In the workshops I do, I will commonly use the example of driving in traffic and ask them, "What do you typically think or do in this situation?" The most common response from my audiences is that they say the other person is a jerk. At that point, I'll ask: "Do you know if the motives behind their actions are jerk-ish motives?" To which they will generally reply with something along the lines of, "Yes. Because only jerks do jerk things, and that was a jerk thing to do." This perspective clearly feels right and justifiable to them. They are thinking, "This person is not following order and is disrespecting me; thus, they must be a jerk." They have a hard time creating space for any alternative explanations.

Second, an inward mindset is self-protective. Not letting someone into my lane when in traffic protects my need for fairness and respect. Approaching my team wondering whether they will fulfill my "me needs" leads me to engage in behaviors that ease my anxieties, but not necessarily those of my teammates. And when teaching, if I focus more on "me needs" than my audience's "they needs," I will feel more certain that the "me needs" will get fulfilled.

Third, our inward mindset generally operates below the level of our consciousness. We enter every social interaction falling somewhere along the continuum between inward and outward. Rarely do we take the time to be intentional about our mindset before or during these interactions. When we get in the car to drive on the freeway, get assigned to a new team, or get asked to teach a class, we rarely think through and choose the degree to which we are going to care about "me needs" as opposed to their "they needs." It just happens.

Fourth, an inward mindset means that we have a narrow window of tolerance for our "me needs" not getting met. Because of this narrow window of tolerance, people with an inward mindset are highly sensitive to whether others are accommodating to them and their needs. If they perceive that others are not accommodating, they are quick to be critical and judgmental, and respond in a manner designed to ensure their needs get met, even if it comes at the expense of others. And when those with an inward mindset are hypersensitive to the meeting of their own needs, it is difficult for them to be sensitive to and attune to the needs of others.

Fifth, an inward mindset is not very cognitive and emotionally sophisticated. With an inward mindset we take on a very narrow view of the world, which is that it revolves around us. This closes us off, cognitively and emotionally, from connecting with and considering other points of view. I am confident in saying that any human atrocity or victimization—think slavery, the Holocaust, genocides, robbery, harassment, rape, and bullying, to name a few—is always founded on an inward mindset.

Sixth, because of all of these reasons, an inward mindset is evidence that our altitude on our Being Side is not very high. If we want to *become better*, we are going to have to widen our window of tolerance for our "me needs" not getting met, which will allow us to be more sensitive to others' "they needs," putting us in a better position for creating value for others.

Outward Mindset

People with an outward mindset have internal programming that allows them to be open and sensitive to others' "they needs." The general result of this programming is that they tend to see others as being just as important as themselves, which allows them to more readily treat them as people, not objects.

There are five aspects of this mindset that are important to understand.

First, an outward mindset is not self-protective. It is value-creating. Consider orchestra conductors. Conductors with inward mindsets are primarily concerned with whether their musicians are playing up to standard. And, being insensitive to the musicians' needs, they will be quick to get angry when the orchestra doesn't play well and be inclined to make demands that are convenient for themselves, regardless of whether those demands are convenient for the musicians. But an orchestra conductor with an outward mindset is going to be more concerned about whether each musician is playing up to their *potential*. The conductor will try to create a culture where the musicians don't operate in fear but with an excitement for creating beautiful music. This latter approach may be more difficult for the conductor, but it will ultimately lead to both a better experience and better music. For more on this, I recommend the book *The Art of Possibility* by Rosamund Stone Zander and Benjamin Zander.

People with an
outward mindset have internal
programming that allows them
to be open and sensitive
to others' "they needs."

_____

Second, people with an outward mindset have a wide window of tolerance for their "me needs" not being met. By not being hypersensitive to the fulfillment of their own needs, their body's nervous system has the capacity to look beyond themselves and get in touch with others' needs and perspectives.

Third, an outward mindset generally operates below our level of consciousness. For the vast majority of their interactions with others, those with an outward mindset automatically and nonconsciously approach those interactions with a certain amount of space left for others' "they needs," usually a larger space than that of those with an inward mindset.

Fourth, an outward mindset is very cognitively and emotionally sophisticated. It takes a lot of this sophistication to be able to put off our "me needs" and give weight and credence to others' "they needs," particularly in situations where the "they needs" run counter to our "me needs."

An important point to make here is that having an outward mindset does not mean we have to neglect our "me needs." Yes, people with an outward mindset create greater space for others' "they needs," but they also have the cognitive and emotional sophistication to create a healthy balance between "me needs" and "they needs." People with an outward mindset recognize that they cannot continually create value for others if their personal tank is not full. Thus, they possess the ability to create healthy boundaries, which helps them ensure that their necessary "me needs" are met so that they have the capacity to create space for "they needs."

Fifth, because of all these reasons, an outward mindset is evidence that the altitude on our Being Side is high. It is an indication that we are primarily disposed to operate in value-creation mode and stay in it despite anxieties around our "me needs" being met. And importantly, from my study of people with inward and outward mindsets, I have come to believe it is only possible to truly love and care for others if we have an outward mindset.

Key Discoveries

In summary, our internal operating system has programming related to how we navigate the tension and pressure between fulfilling our "me needs" and others' "they needs." If our operating system steers us toward satisfying "me needs" over "they needs" in performance situations, that suggests that we have more of an inward mindset. But if the reverse is true, that suggests we have more of an outward mindset.

Applications for Leadership

I think one of the hardest shifts for leaders to make in their career is moving from individual contributor to leader. In fact, it is my experience that most people in leadership positions have not made this shift well. So if you are struggling in changing roles, you are not alone.

A big part of navigating this shift effectively involves developing more of an outward mindset. When we are individual contributors, we are often expected and encouraged to focus predominantly on the "me needs" associated with getting our job done. But when we move into leadership positions, a necessary aspect of these positions is to be a steward of others' "they needs."

What I observe is that many leaders are much more concerned about their "me needs" than their employees' "they needs." But if you study the most effective leaders, you will find a common theme: They all take a human-centric approach to their leadership, seeking to create an environment where their people can grow and thrive.

13

The Value of Understanding the Mindset Framework

So much of our life is dictated by our mindsets.
So much of it! Of how we think, we shall become.
LANA (STAGE NAME OF CATHERINE JOY PERRY)

FROM MY PERSONAL EXPERIENCE, as well as from working with thousands of people on their mindsets, I have found that there are three significant benefits to understanding the mindset framework.

The first is that it helps deepen our self-awareness.

In chapter 7, we focused on the adult development levels framework to give you a general sense of your Being Side altitude. But in the preceding mindset chapters, we leveraged the mindset framework to help you gain a deeper and more nuanced understanding of the wiring of your internal operating system, and the degree to which you are programmed for value creation as opposed to self-protection across different contexts.

For me, one of the most powerful aspects of the mindset framework is that it has given me labels and descriptions to investigate and evaluate my internal operating system. Without having these labels and descriptions, it was impossible for me to introspect about my mindsets, and I proceeded through life assuming they were the ideal ones to have. But when I gained an understanding of this mindset framework, I had the ability to really look in the mirror. And what I found was that I had all four of the self-protective mindsets. That wasn't easy to sit with, but it helped me better see that my typical mode of operation was serving me in self-protective ways, but was also holding me back from my ambitions and aspirations to create value. I quickly learned that if I wanted to *become better*, I would need to upgrade my internal operating system by elevating my mindsets.

So, if you are anything like me and have found that you do not have the ideal mindsets, welcome to "the club." In my experience working with people on their mindsets, I have learned that most people have an internal operating system with wiring that causes them to struggle with navigating at least one of the four tensions connected to the different sets of mindsets. And remember, across the over 50,000 people who have taken my mindset assessment, only 2.5 percent are in the top quartile for all four sets of mindsets. This means that most of us have some self-protective wiring built into our operating system, which is what we should expect given that so few people operate in Mind 3.0.

I have also learned that different groups of individuals tend to struggle with certain specific tensions. For example, leaders tend to struggle the most with a fixed mindset because they generally feel a lot of pressure to look good. People who identify as experts often have more of a closed mindset because admitting that they don't know something or are wrong would go against their identity as an expert. People who are in Mind 1.0 generally have a prevention mindset because they are wired to stay safe and comfortable and want to avoid the discomfort and hassle of problems. And younger adults often struggle more with an inward mindset than those who have more life experience.

Across the over 50,000 people who have taken my mindset assessment, only 2.5 percent are in the top quartile for all four sets of mindsets.

───────────────

The second benefit of understanding this mindset framework builds off a deeper level of self-awareness: It helps us get clear on what reprogramming we need, which will bring precision to the next steps in our *becoming better* journey.

In my own case, I used to think that my self-protective mindsets were normal, justified, and even ideal. But upon learning about these mindsets, I immediately had clarity on some of the changes I needed to make.

I hope you now feel clearer on some of the internal operating system upgrades that you might need to *become better*. Consider these questions:

- For a growth mindset: Do you need to widen your window of tolerance for failing and looking bad so that you can focus more deeply on learning and growing?

- For an open mindset: Do you need to widen your window of tolerance for being wrong or admitting you are wrong so that you can focus more deeply on finding truth and thinking optimally?

- For a promotion mindset: Do you need to widen your window of tolerance for problems and mistakes so that you can focus more deeply on fulfilling your purpose and reaching an aspirational destination?

- For an outward mindset: Do you need to widen your window of tolerance for falling behind so that you can focus more deeply on lifting others?

The third benefit of understanding this mindset framework is that it helps us better understand what it means to have "character." At the beginning of the book, I identified our Being Side as being connected to our character. The mindset framework adds depth to this connection. It helps us understand that character is about the degree to which we possess the wiring to operate in value-creation mode when there is tension and pressure to move into self-protection mode.

When I first came to understand character in this way, it hit me like a ton of bricks. In fact, it still does. This is because I used to see myself as someone with "high character." I pride myself on being someone who strives to be kind, be ethical, and live up to my commitments. But connecting character to the degree to which I am wired for value creation as opposed to self-protection, I now realize that my character is not as high as I once thought. This is because I have recognized that I have self-protective tendencies that limit my character and are holding me back from being the person I want to become. But the good news for me, and for you, is that our *becoming better* journey is never done, and we can upgrade our internal operating system to *become better*.

But before we get into how we upgrade our internal operating system, we first need to spend a couple of chapters deepening our understanding of why some people come to possess self-protective wiring in the first place so that we can better understand how to rise above such wiring.

Key Discoveries

If an organization I am working with has invited its leaders or employees to take my Personal Mindset Assessment, without fail I will have someone comment about how they didn't like their results.

I understand this. I've been there myself, and learning that my mindsets weren't as high-quality as I thought was a tough pill to swallow. But swallowing that pill got me motivated to work on elevating my mindsets, which has ultimately been life-changing and life-elevating.

I don't know how your Personal Mindset Assessment results turned out, but I hope you have already started to see the benefits of awakening to your mindsets. I hope that you

- have deepened your self-awareness,

- have greater clarity on where you can upgrade to become a better version of yourself, and

- can more accurately determine your current level of character and more fully see how you can elevate it.

Applications for Leadership

When I work for organizations, not only do the leaders and employees get their own individual results from my Personal Mindset Assessment, but I will aggregate their results up to the collective level to produce a mindset report for the group as a whole. I have now done this with over 300 organizations and groups. Let me share two primary things that I have learned from this experience.

First, I have learned that there are two common profiles: Mind 1.0 and Mind 2.0. Organizations with predominately Mind 1.0 leaders and employees generally have high levels of fixed mindsets, open mindsets, prevention mindsets, and outward mindsets. These results correspond to programming for self-protective safety, comfort, and belonging. In these cases, more prominent open and outward mindsets are mechanisms that help people feel more safe, comfortable, and like they fit in. Organizations with many Mind 2.0 leaders and employees have high fixed mindsets, moderate open mindsets, high promotion mindsets, and moderate outward mindsets. These results correspond to programming for making progress. These individuals are very results-oriented, which makes them less focused on valuing people and ideas and more focused on not failing while in the pursuit of short-term goals.

Do you think one of these profiles matches what we would find in your organization?

Second, I have learned that these collective mindset results allow me to get a really clear understanding of the fears that exist in an organization's culture that are holding the organization back from moving toward its potential.

- If an organization has high fixed mindsets, there are cultural fears of failing or looking bad. And it is likely that the organization struggles with creativity, innovation, and staying current.

- If an organization has high closed mindsets, there are cultural fears of not being right or having all of the answers. It is likely that it struggles with psychological safety.

- If an organization has high prevention mindsets, there are cultural fears of having problems or making mistakes. The organization likely struggles with micromanagement, bureaucracy, energy, and agility.

- If an organization has high inward mindsets, it is a sign that there is a lot of competition in the organization, and people have fears of falling behind. It is likely the organization has a siloed, selfish, and toxic culture.

Do you know what cultural fears your organization has that are holding it back from creating more value?

14

How Trauma Impacts
Our Being Side

*Who you are becoming is more
important than who you have been.*
UNKNOWN

A FEW YEARS ago, I was completely uninformed about trauma, both personally and professionally.

From a personal perspective, if you had asked me if I had trauma in my past, I would have defensively answered, "No!" To justify my answer, I would have explained that I had not been exposed to an extreme event, I had not been assaulted or physically abused, and I saw my parents as being supportive. They went to almost every basketball game I ever played.

From a professional perspective, I had come to understand that our mindsets play a critical role in how our body's nervous system dictates how we process, interpret, and navigate our world. And I wanted to better understand what might cause someone's nervous system to take on the more self-protective mindsets.

At that point in time, I was doing one-on-one vertical development coaching with a few different executive teams, and a pattern was revealing itself. As I asked executives where they thought their self-protective mindsets came from, almost all of them discussed aspects of their upbringing. For example, one executive talked about how he never felt he could please his dad, and because of that he has lived his life seeking the approval of others. Another executive talked about how his parents divorced when he was young. His dad wasn't around, and his mom did not provide him with much of anything beyond basic needs. Making this connection between his upbringing and his mindsets, he felt that because he hadn't been recognized by his parents, he has been driven to obtain accolades and recognition in his professional life.

Hearing stories like these got me wondering if past trauma could potentially explain why people develop more self-protective mindsets, so I started reading almost any book about trauma that I could get my hands on.

This is when I read Bessel van der Kolk's book *The Body Keeps the Score* and learned about EMDR, as I discussed in chapter 6.

Still unsure if I had trauma in my past, I called up an EMDR therapist in my area to ask about her services and if she thought EMDR could help me even if there was no past trauma. She explained that EMDR could help me refine my body's nervous system and work through mental blocks that I may have that are holding me back in my profession and relationships. Seeing no harm in trying it out, as well as seeing it as an opportunity to learn more about the connection between trauma and mindsets, I started working with this therapist.

The first step of my therapy was to identify areas of my life that were not ideal. Having identified those, we started to dive into the reasons why I was struggling in those areas. Essentially, we were looking for mental blocks that were holding me back and exploring where these blocks came from and why they existed. For every block that we uncovered, my therapist guided me to dig into my past, which was something I had largely avoided before then. At first, I felt my walls of resistance coming up. But I was so confident that we wouldn't find anything significant in my past that I decided to be a "good sport" and let her dig around.

As she guided this digging, my therapist asked a lot of questions about my parents. Initially, I was always quick to tell her that my parents were great, they were very supportive, and I always had the things I needed. But what both she and I started to discover was that while my parents went to my basketball games and provided me with the basic necessities, they were emotionally neglectful. They rarely, if ever, attuned to my emotional needs or supported me in difficult and stressful situations. In fact, my therapist homed in on two major scars from my past. The first was when I was five years old. My parents got into a massive argument, and my dad threatened to leave my mom. I can still vividly remember seeing him packing his suitcase. I was bawling my eyes out and was so scared. After the event, neither of my parents came to comfort me. I was left to deal with those hard emotions alone. Similarly, when I was 10, my brother-in-law, someone I looked up to as a brother, unexpectedly passed away. Upon hearing the news, I broke down. I cried for hours under a blanket on our couch. My parents never tried to comfort me. Again, they left me alone when I was emotionally distressed.

Upon uncovering these wounds, it became clear to me and my therapist that throughout my childhood, I had been emotionally neglected. This was alarming to me because in *The Body Keeps the Score*, Bessel van der Kolk writes that emotional neglect can be as harmful as physical abuse, if not more so. But learning and acknowledging this emotional neglect was also liberating and eye-opening. It was liberating because it opened the door for me to do some healing work that needed to be done. And it was eye-opening because it helped me see the connections between my trauma and my self-protective mindsets.

I ended up working with my therapist for two years, and it was a life-healing and life-transforming experience. I was able to help my body's nervous system heal and start functioning better, which has helped me operate more in Mind 3.0, as a value creator, as I will explain later in this chapter.

Through this process and through my own dive into neuroscience research, I have come to learn the neuroscience associated with how trauma affects our body's internal operating system. I want to share this science with you because it will play a significant role when we start discussing how we can upgrade our operating system.

What Is Trauma and How Prevalent Is It?

Psychologists estimate that over 70 percent of people have experienced trauma in their lives. While this estimation comes from a variety of sources, one primary source is connected to studies on adverse childhood experiences (ACEs). For these studies, researchers compiled a list of 10 impactful childhood experiences with trauma, including physical injury by a parent, humiliation by a parent, sexual abuse, emotional neglect, physical neglect, exposure to domestic violence, exposure to drug use, being raised in a home with someone who was mentally ill, and more. Researchers found that 64 percent of people have experienced at least one ACE before turning 18, and 17 percent have experienced at least four by that age.

As you can imagine, the more ACEs one experiences, the greater the impact on the person. For those who have experienced four or more ACEs, researchers have found that compared to those with no ACEs, their life expectancy is 20 years shorter. They also are

- 30 times more likely to commit suicide.
- 7 times more likely to suffer from alcoholism.
- 14 times more likely to be a victim of violence.
- 15 times more likely to commit violence.
- 20 times more likely to be incarcerated.

If 64 percent of people have experienced trauma before they are 18, it is easy to infer that at least 70 percent of adults have experienced it, which has surely had an impact on their internal operating system and how they navigate their world.

But ACEs aren't exactly the same as trauma. So what is trauma?

Trauma is most commonly spoken of as a negative experience one lives through. But trauma is best defined not as what happens to us, but by the impact our experiences have on us.

Simply stated, trauma is a psychological wounding. More specifically, trauma is any nervous system adaptation that is the result of hurtful or jarring experiences we have had. These adaptations are the body's natural way of protecting us in extreme moments of stress and helping us avoid similar stress and pain in the future. While such adaptations are helpful for limiting our pain and ensuring our safety in the short-term aftermath of a stressful experience, they generally impede how one processes and operates in their world outside of the context of trauma.

For example, recall my coaching client, Tom, the executive who was a veteran and former EMT. He had experienced significant stressful experiences in his past roles that caused his body's nervous system to become hypersensitive to preventing and avoiding problems. While this adaptation has surely helped him deal with or avoid the stress and pain he experienced in the battlefield or when serving as an EMT, it was also getting in the way of his being an effective leader in a business context.

Defining trauma by neurological impact is helpful for at least two reasons. First, it explains why two people can experience a similar negative event, yet it affects one person much more than the other. Second, it forces us to connect with our body's nervous system and how it regulates our internal operating system.

We Have a Stress Response System Built into Our Nervous System

To more deeply understand what trauma is and its effects on our body, it is helpful to explore an important part of our nervous system: our stress response system. As was mentioned in chapter 2, one of the primary jobs of our nervous system is to protect us and keep us alive. Our stress response system plays a major role in this process. Let me try to bring this to life.

If you have ever stood at the edge of a tall cliff, what was your body telling you to do? If your stress response system was working as it should, it was making changes to your body to protect you by getting away from the cliff. Specifically, it was sending stress hormones into your body to activate an enhanced ability to respond to threats. Your nerves were more on edge; your heart started to race, taking more oxygen into your body; your pupils dilated to let in more light, allowing you to see better; and your palms started to sweat, which enhances your grip if you need to grab onto a ledge or use a tool. Your stress response system can do some pretty cool things to help keep us alive.

Now, something we need to recognize is that just as everyone differs in terms of their muscular strength, each of our stress response systems differs in strength or ability to take on stress. Some people's stress response systems can healthily absorb and process a lot of stress, while other people have a weaker system that makes them less stress-tolerant. I introduced this idea previously when I explained the concept of the window of tolerance.

To understand the impact of trauma on the body, we need to consider difficult situations where the stress exceeds our stress response system's ability to deal with it. In such situations our response system will go to extreme measures to protect us and keep us alive. These measures generally take the form of either extreme overdrive or almost complete deactivation. While these extreme measures help us survive the tough moment, their fallout leaves lasting neurological changes that impact our internal operating system beyond the context of the stress. While these changes can be seen as beneficial as they are generally self-protective in nature and designed to prevent us from experiencing further trauma, they are evidence that psychological wounding has occurred.

Because we know that stress response systems vary in strength, that means that people with weaker response systems are more prone to experience the psychological wounding that leads to self-protective neurological adaptations. Known factors that play a role in the strength and resilience of our stress response system include the level of support we have from others in the immediate aftermath of the traumatic experience, our genetic makeup, our self-regulatory abilities and coping strategies, and our age when the experience occurs, among other factors.

Putting these pieces together, we can now explain why two people who experience the same traumatic experience, like combat or a car wreck, might respond differently to it, with one being more psychologically wounded than the other. Trauma is not what happens to us—it is the neurological adaptations that occur as a result of experiencing stress beyond our body's capacity to deal with stress.

Momentarily I will explain the specific neurological adaptations that occur as a result of this overload. But first, it is worth noting that there is a common categorization of different forms of trauma that helps us identify the types of experiences that lead to the neurological adaptations that we are calling "trauma."

Basic Categorization of Trauma

Trauma experts generally point to three types of experiences or situations that commonly result in self-protective neurological adaptations. They are the basic categorizations of trauma.

The first category is prenatal trauma. Prenatal trauma is neurological changes that are the result of the stress that a fetus may experience directly or indirectly through its mother. Direct prenatal trauma may include the effects of the mother's substance abuse, issues with blood supply to the baby, or medical complications while the baby is in utero. Indirect prenatal trauma includes maternal stress or mental health issues that the mother experiences during pregnancy, which may cause hormone imbalances in the fetus and impact neurological development.

The second category is "Big T" trauma. "Big T" is generally described as experiencing a single major traumatic event.

The third is "Little t" trauma, the experience of consistent and possibly unpredictable stress over time.

These latter two categories do not have distinct boundaries and commonly blur together. But the reason the categorization is helpful is because it helps us recognize that traumatic neurological adaptations can be caused by a variety of factors and in a number of different ways.

While all this helps us better understand the most common causes of trauma, recall that stressful experiences impact people differently contingent upon the strength of their stress-response systems. So it is less important to consider the cause of the trauma than how dramatic the neurological adaptations are as a result of the stressful experience.

As an example, in my study of trauma I have observed that physical abuse is generally classified as "Big T" trauma, and emotional neglect, a passive and commonly ongoing form of abuse, is generally classified as "Little t." Despite these different categorizations, research has found that both predictably lead to negative neurological adaptations of similar magnitude.

Trauma Leads to Self-Protective Wiring

So, what is the impact of trauma on one's internal operating system? To answer this question, we'll start at the surface level and then dive deeper into the neuroscience of trauma.

It should not surprise us that the basic negative consequence of trauma is that it causes one's internal operating system to become more wired for self-protection. Remember, the primary job of our body's nervous system is to protect us and keep us alive. When we experience pain associated with a traumatic situation or experience, of course our body wants to avoid experiencing any future such pain. And why wouldn't it? So, our body makes adjustments to the nervous system in a manner that will hopefully prevent us from experiencing that situation and/or pain in the future. Thus, trauma is one explanation for why some people operate at lower mind levels and have more self-protective mindsets.

After I awoke to my trauma—being emotionally neglected by my parents—it became clear to me that the impact of this neglect was the development of my inward mindset and avoidant attachment style. My body learned at a rather young age that I was alone for the meeting of my emotional needs. Thus, my nervous system developed self-protective wiring to help ensure that those needs were met in the future, and my internal operating system became programmed to be much more concerned about my "me needs" than others' "they needs." Also, my operating system became programmed to not trust or expect that others will meet my emotional needs. Thus, when I'm in a relationship, my body is wired to avoid closeness and reliance on others. Such programming protects me from reexperiencing the pain of aloneness I felt as a child. But it also has been an obstacle to me being the partner, parent, and leader I desire to be.

Before I awakened to my trauma story, I knew I was not yet the person that I wanted to be, nor did I have the relationships that I wanted to have. I wanted to become better. But at the same time, I didn't have a clear understanding of why I possessed this gap between who I was and who I wanted to be. After getting in touch with my trauma background, however, not only did I have a clear answer for this gap, but I also gained clarity on what I needed to do to close it: heal from my past trauma and rewire my internal operating system.

As I continue to coach leaders, I am observing more and more how their own past trauma causes gaps between who they are and who they want to be. Let me give you a couple of examples from my coaching clients. I have changed their names to protect their identities. For each, notice how their past trauma has caused them to develop self-protective programming that protects them from pain and discomfort when stress occurs, yet holds them back from creating value in the present.

In my coaching program, I start by having my clients identify an aspiration for their leadership, and then we leverage that aspiration as the goal for the coaching process. Given what I have learned about vertical development, I recognize that if they are ever going to make transformational progress toward their aspirations, I need to get a sense of any self-protective programming that is preventing them from doing so. This means that my coaching program involves a deep introspective dive, which is where these examples come from.

I brought up Paul in chapter 4. He is the executive in his 50s who struggles to take initiative. His aspiration was to become better at taking initiative. He told me he is great at taking direction from others, like his CEO, but has a hard time coming up with a plan on his own and then taking action on it. (Honestly, when he first told me this, it threw me for a loop. I was shocked hearing this from an executive.) After asking him for an example of how he has struggled in this area, he said, "Even now, as an adult, when I go to buy a new car, I still feel like I need to get my parents' permission." Wanting to understand this more, I asked him where he thought this reluctance to take personal initiative came from. His answer was, "When I was a child, I couldn't do anything to please my father." He was raised in a situation where, when he took initiative, he was commonly met with disapproval from the person he most wanted approval from. Hence, his internal operating system became wired to stop taking initiative because he did not want to be met with disapproval. While his internal wiring makes sense given his past, it is something that is holding him back from being more of a value creator.

Next, let me tell you about Mandy. Before I started coaching Mandy, her boss and CEO, Rick, wanted to explain why he was signing her up for coaching. Rick told me that Mandy has two parts of her job: She needs to make sales herself, something she excels at; but she also needs to manage and develop a team of sales reps, something that she struggles with. And to warn me about how much Mandy struggles with her team, Rick told me that she has a license plate cover that says, "People Suck." When I started coaching her, she admitted that she was not a great manager, but she wanted to become better. Right away, it was clear that she had trust issues.

She naturally and automatically assumed that her team members "sucked," and she was reluctant to pass work off to them because she held tightly to two interrelated beliefs. The first belief was that if she had her employees do the work, then she would inevitably have to redo everything. The second was that if she did the work herself, it would get done right and more quickly.

If there is a gap between who we currently are and who we want to become, trauma might be a key cause and explanation for that gap.

———————————————

Recognizing that she struggles with trust and delegation, I asked her where she thought these struggles stemmed from. Immediately, she went on to tell me that she had lost one of her children and that was one of the hardest things she has had to live through. In telling me about the loss of her child, which she didn't go into depth on, she also implied that another person was to blame for the child's death. This loss was clearly weighing on her, and I could see how this experience damaged her trust in humanity.

Upon hearing this story, it became clear to me that this experience led her to develop self-protective wiring about the untrustworthiness of people. Given her loss, this wiring seems justifiable and was surely designed to protect her from future pain. But at the same time, this self-protective wiring was holding her back from being the leader and person she ideally wanted to be.

I wish I could tell you that these examples are uncommon. But from my experience, they are not. And perhaps I shouldn't be shocked given that 64 percent of people have experienced at least one adverse childhood experience in their life.

If there is a pattern that I find most common across my coaching, it is this: It is common for leaders to have experienced some form of neglect as a child that made them feel unseen or unvalued. As a result of these childhood experiences, their internal operating system has responded by developing programming that makes them seek being seen or valued. Sometimes this shows up as being people-pleasers, and other times as hard-charging "doers" focused on results, wins, accolades, and prestige, as opposed to effective leaders.

If there is a gap between who we currently are and who we want to become, trauma might be a key cause and explanation for it.

The Impact of Trauma at a Neurological Level

While it makes sense that people who experience trauma will become more self-protective, I have found it incredibly helpful to understand the specific neurological changes that result from the psychological wounding of trauma.

Neuroscientists have found that there are three brain networks that are responsible for processing our environment and determining our response to it. They are the salience network, the default mode network, and the central executive network. These networks are where our mindsets' neural connections reside.

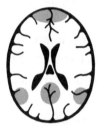

Salience Network
Our brain's emotional hub. Responsible for switching our processing between the Default Mode Network and Central Executive Network.

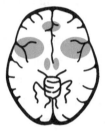

Default Mode Network
Our home of non-conscious processing. Assists in emotional regulation.

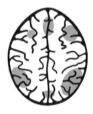

Central Executive Network
Our home of conscious processing and rational thought.

The salience network is the brain's emotional hub, made up of our amygdala, insula, anterior cingulate cortex, and ventrolateral prefrontal cortex. It has three primary jobs. The first is being our signal processor. It detects signals from our environment and determines which are relevant and in need of greater attention. Second, being the brain's emotional hub and primary interpretation center, it then interprets those signals and assigns meaning and feelings to them. The salience network's third job is to initiate behavioral responses. This means that it needs to determine which of the two other brain networks needs to get involved to most efficiently and effectively respond to the signals it processed.

The salience network gets the default mode network involved when it determines that conscious processing is not needed, as the default mode network is where our nonconscious processing takes place. It is comprised of our ventromedial prefrontal cortex and the posterior cingulate cortex. As the network involved in our nonconscious processing, it is performing several important tasks below our conscious awareness. First, it is our autopilot. Have you ever driven from one place to another, not really paying attention during the journey, and then wondered how you got there? That was your default mode network doing its thing. Second, it uses self-information, like feelings from our body, autobiographical memories, and our visions of the future to nonconsciously direct us toward actions to meet our body's needs, wants, and interests. Third, it plays a role in how we navigate socially, specifically by dictating the degree to which we pick up on the emotions of others, demonstrate empathy, and operate with morality.

But if after processing its signals the salience network determines that conscious processing is needed, it will get the central executive network involved. The central executive network involves the dorsolateral prefrontal cortex and posterior parietal cortex and is responsible for our cognitive control processes like attentional control and rational problem-solving and decision-making.

We tend to think that our central executive network is our "driver" because it is the only network whose operation is something we are conscious of. And, yes, while our salience network can make our central executive network the driver in certain circumstances, for the most part the autopilot of our default mode network is driving the show. This is another reason why psychologists have said that 90 percent of our thinking, feeling, judging, and acting are driven by our nonconscious, automatic processes.

Ideally, all three of these brain networks will work effectively together. When they work as a cohesive team, it enables us to accurately encode and navigate our situations in a manner that is best suited for that situation. When they do not work cohesively, we become prone to misencode our situations, inhibiting our ability to navigate our environments effectively.

To bring this to life, let me share an experience we recently observed with an extended family member. I'll call him Chris. Chris has been through a lot in his life. At a young age, his parents divorced. While he was raised by both of his parents, his mom had mental health challenges, was overly critical of Chris, and was not very loving or affectionate. As you can imagine, Chris has some scars as a result of his upbringing.

In this particular situation, Chris, who is now in his 40s, was with a group of family members setting up for an event. Of all the people there, Chris was being the least helpful and was negatively impacting the morale of the group. In this moment, Chris's dad, in a straightforward yet non-aggressive way, asked Chris to be a little more positive and helpful. Chris's response to this request was that he shut down and sulkingly walked off. We did not see him for the rest of the night.

Given that Chris's response seemed to be an overreaction, it is an indication that his brain networks were not working effectively together. He experienced receiving feedback, something that did not put him in any sort of danger, as being an attack that left him feeling unsafe. So to protect himself, he left. I can imagine that if his brain networks were working more effectively together, rather than walking away he would have taken the feedback as an opportunity to adjust and improve, change his attitude, and become more helpful in setting up for the event.

This example helps demonstrate what neuroscientists have learned about the impact of trauma on the three brain networks. When the three networks work effectively together, they allow one to see safe things as being safe and dangerous things as being dangerous. But when our brain networks are not working effectively together, a common result of experiencing trauma, our brain becomes prone to see safe things as dangerous (like corrective feedback from a parent) and dangerous things as safe.

More specifically, neuroscientists have found that trauma generally results in one of two different adaptations in how these brain networks function, both of which primarily involve how the salience network and default mode network work together. Let's explore both adaptations.

Adaptation 1: Hypervigilance

One way that the body adapts to trauma is to adjust its wiring to be more sensitive to potential threats. The body becomes hypervigilant, or more carefully watchful for potential danger to an excessive degree.

At a brain network level, the hypervigilant adaptation that occurs is twofold. First, the salience network, the home of our signal processing and emotions, becomes overactive. It starts to pick up on signals of potential danger that it would not have picked up on before and becomes more prone to assign "danger" to these signals. Second, the default mode network becomes diminished in its ability to healthily regulate the salience network. The result of these adaptations is that people who are hypervigilant tend to interpret signals that should normally be considered safe as being unsafe.

Hypervigilance is an ideal adaptation to trauma if the individual continues to live in the context where the trauma occurred. It serves to protect them from reoccurring or future trauma. I mentioned earlier that my wife had the experience of watching the movie *It* as a young child. This was a traumatic experience for her because it altered her body's nervous system in a way that has made her hypervigilant. Even now, as an adult, her body is so hypersensitive to seeing clowns that when she sees a picture of a clown, something that clearly does not put her in any danger, her body interprets that picture as a sign that she is unsafe. Her salience network is quick to react and activate her stress response system for protection. Simultaneously, her default mode network is unable to effectively step in and help regulate her salience network by telling it, "That is only a picture, you don't need to overreact here."

Another fairly common example is with military personnel who have seen combat experience. When they experience combat situations where their life is continually threatened, their body's nervous system is likely to become more hypersensitive to potential threats. This is going to help keep them alive in combat situations. But the hypervigilance that serves them well in combat contexts generally hinders their ability to effectively interact with their world when they return home and are in an environment where their life is not continually threatened. It is common for military personnel to be more prone to see others in their environment as potential threats, be quicker to react in aggression, be triggered by loud noises or sudden movement, and be unable to unwind.

While hypervigilance is a well-intended adaptation with our safety and protection in mind, it ultimately causes one's internal operating system to operate at lower levels of cognitive and emotional sophistication. People with hypervigilant wiring have narrower windows of tolerance, operate at lower vertical development altitudes, and have more and stronger self-protective mindsets. They are prone to suspicion, mistrust, and carrying negative expectations for the future. They overly engage in safety-seeking thinking and behaviors. They struggle with anxiety. And, they also tend to develop a more anxious attachment style in their relationships. Specifically, they are often hypersensitive to any signals that their partner or other loved ones will abandon or reject them, which causes them to struggle to feel secure with others.

While hypervigilant neural adaptations can be severe enough to be debilitating, they generally are not. They simply reduce one's ability to effectively navigate their environments compared to others who are not wired that way. Let me give you another example that came up from a woman in one of my workshops. I'll call her Tina.

Tina is a good and respected employee in her organization, and for many things, she is seen and valued as a go-to expert. But she has some struggles related to hypervigilance that her peers do not. For some context, Tina was raised in a home where her parents were inconsistent with their love, affection, and praise. On occasion, her parents were very warm and loving, but most of the time were the exact opposite. They could be quick to anger, highly critical, and cold. For Tina, she didn't know which parents she was going to get day by day. So, she became overly sensitive to any cues from her parents indicating that they were in their cold state or warm state.

While this oversensitivity helped her navigate her childhood, it is proving to be a hurdle in her work interactions. She admitted to me that she has challenges operating in a job that is mostly virtual and where most communication occurs via email, a context where she cannot pick up on the nonverbal cues of others. Specifically, she is always anxious about email communications from her boss. Without having nonverbal cues, she is unable to tell whether her boss is being warm or cold. And her hypervigilance is prone to interpret her boss as being cold, which is rarely if ever the case. To help navigate this context more effectively, Tina has asked her boss to include emojis in all of her communication to help her feel more secure in her interpretations of her boss's state, tone, and intent.

Altogether, hypervigilance is a neural adaptation to stressful situations that makes one's internal operating system programmed for self-protection, causing them to operate at a less-than-ideal altitude on their Being Side and hindering their ability to be a value creator.

Adaptation 2: Dissociation

Another way that the body adapts to trauma is to reduce its ability to feel the pain of trauma. This neural adaptation is called dissociation, and neurologically it is the opposite of hypervigilance.

When some people experience trauma, particularly situations with significant physical or emotional pain, if the pain of that circumstance is more than the body can tolerate, our nervous system will go to the extreme measure of cutting off our connection to our feelings and emotions. While dissociation helps us survive the moment, this disconnection leaves long-lasting diminishment of our ability to connect with our emotions and feelings moving forward.

At the brain network level, we experience dissociation when the default mode network becomes overactive, overregulating the salience network. This imbalance prevents emotions and feelings from coming online to the degree that they would with healthier brain functionality.

I have come to learn that the trauma-induced neural adaptation that I have struggled with is dissociation. For me, having parents who were poor at connecting with my emotions and helping me effectively navigate them left me alone to figure out how to deal with my big emotions. To help with this, my body decided that the best way to deal with my emotions was to not feel them. At times, this can help me because I don't feel the pain that others might in difficult or challenging situations, allowing me to be resilient.

While I have seen my emotional stability and resilience as a strength, Brené Brown has written, "When we stop feeling hurt by cruelty, we lose our ability to connect." This resonates with me in two ways. First, while having diminished ability to connect to difficult feelings means I don't struggle with them, it also means that I have less ability to connect with the positive. Second, I do recognize that my dissociative wiring prevents me from connecting with others in the way I would like. I have learned that my body is programmed with a narrow window of tolerance for connecting with others at an emotional level as a self-protective safety mechanism, manifesting as an avoidant attachment style.

But the good news is that through my work with my trauma therapist, I have seen significant growth in this area. I can tell that I have improved the wiring in my brain. I know this because I am experiencing greater emotional fluctuations between the good and the bad. I do a better job of recognizing, labeling, and communicating my feelings. And I am much more willing to be vulnerable than I have been in the past. I still have a ways to go, but I feel I am heading in the right direction. I feel I have *become better*.

Like hypervigilance, dissociation is a well-intended adaptation that has our safety and protection in mind. But it ultimately causes one's internal operating system to function at lower levels of cognitive and emotional sophistication. People with dissociative wiring have narrower windows of tolerance, are more prone to experience hypoarousal and go into freeze mode, operate at lower vertical development altitudes, and have more and stronger self-protective mindsets. They have a reduced ability to connect with both the emotional and physical sensations in their body, which commonly results in decreased sensitivity to salient signals, diminished interoceptive abilities, body-ownership distortions, and being more vulnerable to abuse. Are you someone who gets uncomfortable with big emotions and tries to quickly move away from them? If so, that might suggest a level of dissociation.

Emotional Intelligence

Before closing out this chapter, I want to spotlight a fascinating insight about our Being Side that only becomes apparent when we understand the neural adaptations of hypervigilance and dissociation. It is connected to one of the most important sets of abilities for navigating our world effectively: emotional intelligence.

Emotional intelligence has been found to be a vital aspect of personal success, largely because it has a huge influence on our ability to effectively navigate the social and relational aspects of our life. Consider the following research findings:

- TalentSmartEQ reports that emotional intelligence is the strongest predictor of performance out of 34 essential workplace skills, explaining 58 percent of success in all types of jobs.

- TalentSmartEQ also reports that employees with high emotional intelligence are more likely to stay calm under pressure, resolve conflict effectively, and respond to coworkers with empathy.

- Daniel Goleman, considered the father of emotional intelligence, has reported that over 80 percent of competencies that differentiate top performers from others are in the domain of emotional intelligence.

- The Hay Group has reported that salespeople with high emotional intelligence produce twice the revenue of those with average or below-average emotional intelligence.

What exactly is emotional intelligence? It is commonly broken down into four skills, two related to our connection with and management of our own emotions (self-awareness and self-management) and two related to our ability to connect with and navigate others' emotions (social awareness and relationship management).

The Four Dimensions of Emotional Intelligence

What neuroscientists have discovered is that the two neural adaptations of trauma, hypervigilance and dissociation, diminish one's capacity for emotional intelligence in unique ways. When people have an internal operating system wired for hypervigilance, their overactive salience network reduces their abilities in self-management (skill #2) and social awareness (skill #3). Hypervigilant people are prone to get so caught up in their own emotions and experiences that it makes it difficult for them to connect with and accurately identify the emotions and perspectives of others.

On the other hand, when people have an internal operating system wired for dissociation, their overactive default mode network reduces their abilities in self-awareness (skill #1) and relationship management (skill #4). Since dissociated people struggle to connect with their own emotions, it is a challenge for them to effectively navigate those of others.

Understanding the neuroscience behind emotional intelligence is powerful because it clearly identifies this quality as a Being Side characteristic, connected directly to the sophistication of our body's internal operating system. This is significant for two reasons. First, it suggests that a major benefit of elevating along our Being Side should be an improvement in our emotional intelligence. I think we would all agree that if we become more emotionally intelligent, we are becoming better. Second, understanding the neuroscience behind emotional intelligence helps us more clearly see that most efforts used to help people improve their emotional intelligence are not ideally suited for the task. Specifically, I have found that most of these efforts focus on horizontal development, which helps people develop Doing Side knowledge and skills associated with emotional intelligence. For example, common efforts involve trainings on how to listen or provide feedback more effectively. While such trainings can help us know what to do and when to do them, it is a completely different thing to get our bodies to actually operate in an emotionally intelligent way in the moments those skills are really needed. Elevating our emotional intelligence requires vertical development efforts that improve our neurofunctioning and lead to a corresponding elevation on our Being Side.

Key Discoveries

In this chapter, we have illuminated some key ideas that culminate in an incredibly beautiful and meaningful takeaway. These ideas are:

- Trauma alters the functionality of our body's nervous system, or internal operating system.

- Specifically, trauma causes our internal operating system to become more wired for self-protection, via either hypervigilance or dissociation.

- The more trauma we experience, the more likely we are to operate from a low altitude on our Being Side.

Yet, there is good news. We can heal from trauma, and as we do, we become less self-protective and elevate along our Being Side. Altogether, the key takeaway is this: *becoming better*, at its core, is ultimately about healing. It is about healing our mind, body, and heart.

Applications for Leadership

Throughout this chapter I have used multiple examples to communicate a core idea related to leadership: Our past trauma can play a significant role in how we show up as leaders.

In fact, I have observed that many people want to be in a position of leadership to help fill holes or voids left by traumatic experiences in their past. For example, I asked one CEO I worked with why he started his business, and his answer was, "To prove others wrong." Another self-aware CEO told me he started his business because he didn't have very good self-esteem, and that winning in business helped him feel of value.

While fear and filling emotional holes can lead some people to do amazing things, like build a successful business, the self-protective motives behind such efforts generally cause these leaders to operate in a manner that leaves a wake of collateral damage behind them.

For both of the CEOs I just identified, they had created a rather toxic work environment where their executive teams were burned out and frustrated with their CEO.

From my experience, past trauma is at the root of the majority of leadership issues, but unfortunately, it is rarely addressed in leadership development efforts.

For more on this, check out my TEDx Talk, "How to Fix Leadership Development."

15

How ADHD Impacts Our Being Side

Too much of the education system orients students toward becoming better thinkers, but there is almost no focus on our capacity to pay attention and cultivate awareness.

JON KABAT-ZINN

FROM STUDYING THE ROLE that past trauma can play in one's leadership, I knew that I had uncovered at least one primary reason why people may operate at lower Being Side altitudes and have more self-protective mindsets. But I was also interested in discovering other possible reasons.

Around the time that I was wrapping up my therapy, Jena and I started to see some behavioral problems with our 10-year-old daughter. They were very clearly emotional regulation issues. Let me try to paint the picture.

There were situations where we needed to set limits for our daughter, like requiring her to complete her homework before a certain time, limiting the amount of treats she could have, or having her go to bed by a certain time. Historically, accepting these boundaries wasn't too big of an issue for her. But we noticed an increasing sensitivity to these boundaries, and there were a few instances where she would push so hard against them that she would lose emotional control. Her body would tense up, she would ball her fists, and freeze in what looked like a fit of rage. We could tell that her nervous system was going what seemed like a thousand miles an hour. As this went from one occurrence to two, to three, to four, we became concerned about a growing pattern. After speaking to our therapist about it, she recommended that we get our daughter tested for ADHD.

At first, this caught us off guard because our daughter is not very hyperactive. But interested in getting her some help and support, we got her tested.

Sure enough, she was diagnosed with ADHD. But what surprised me was that she was diagnosed with what is called ADHD-Combined, a combination of both hyperactive and inattentive symptoms. I had never heard of this before, and it set me on a journey to learn more about ADHD, which has had profound impacts on my family and how I think about vertical development.

What Is ADHD?

ADHD is a neurodevelopmental disorder of self-control and executive functioning that impedes one's self-regulatory abilities. Specifically, people with ADHD struggle with two executive-functioning issues: (1) sustaining attention and action toward a goal or activity amid distractions, and (2) controlling impulses. In his book *12 Principles for Raising a Child with ADHD*, Russell A. Barkley reports that people with ADHD possess executive-functioning deficits of 30 percent compared with people without ADHD.

More specifically, Barkley identifies seven executive-function issues that people with ADHD tend to struggle with. As I introduce these, consider whether they seem like Being Side or Doing Side issues. And consider if you or others close to you struggle with any of them. Remember, most adults who have ADHD do not know that they have it.

Executive Function Issue 1: diminished self-awareness. People with ADHD are less able to attune to their thinking, speaking, feeling, and actions. They are prone to run on autopilot, particularly in situations where it is least effective to do so, like stressful or high-sensory situations. This makes them more distractible and reactive to events, preventing them from being more proactive, thoughtful, and deliberate.

Executive Function Issue 2: diminished inhibition or self-restraint. People with ADHD struggle to pause and think between stimulus and action. This causes them to react in self-protective ways as opposed to being more thoughtful and intentional about operating in a value-creating manner.

Executive Function Issue 3: diminished working memory. We access our working memory when we reach into the past to direct our behavior in the present (hindsight), or when we contemplate a goal or destination for our future and let that guide our behavior (foresight). People with ADHD struggle to connect with both hindsight and foresight. Because they have trouble with hindsight, they have a difficult time learning and adjusting based on past experiences; commonly lose track of what they're supposed to be doing in a given place and time; and are forgetful about directives, rules, and promises. And because they struggle with foresight, they get distracted and sidetracked easily in the moment, have a harder time connecting with long-term goals or a value-creating purpose, and find it hard to be persistent in working toward the fulfillment of a goal or purpose over time. Altogether, they are more prone to react to the whims and emotions of the moment.

Executive Function Issue 4: diminished time management abilities. People with ADHD tend to be blind to time. They struggle to use the passage of time to control their own behaviors. They fail to prepare for deadlines, misestimate how long it may take to do things, and have problems connecting with the consequences of not meeting deadlines. Thus, they often fail to keep time commitments with others.

Executive Function Issue 5: diminished emotional self-control. People with ADHD struggle with emotional restraint, and thus tend to be emotionally reactive. Combined with issues of hindsight, people with ADHD not only tend to be emotionally reactive, but also have a hard time learning from missteps they have made where their emotional reactivity has caused them problems.

Executive Function Issue 6: diminished self-motivation. People with ADHD struggle with completing routine chores or tasks. When faced with these tasks, they seek out more interesting, exciting, or rewarding things to do, activities that are generally more self-interested than value-creating. Further, combining a lack of self-motivation with reduced foresight, people with ADHD struggle to work long, hard, and persistently for large long-term goals or a deep, meaningful purpose. And they will struggle even more if the long-term goals or purpose isn't connected to their own self-serving benefits.

Executive Function Issue 7: diminished self-organization, planning, and problem-solving. People with ADHD struggle to plan things out and problem-solve. This is because they struggle with generating multiple ideas or options to solving a problem, and with figuring out the best sequence of steps for addressing it. As a result, they have trouble working around obstacles.

When people with ADHD experience these issues, it indicates that their current programming is less than ideal. In fact, by identifying these issues, it becomes clear that people with ADHD have a neurological condition that makes them prone to operate at a lower altitude on their Being Side and possess more narrow windows of tolerance, reduced cognitive and emotional sophistication, and self-protective wiring.

If someone has gone undiagnosed with ADHD and they manifest less-than-ideal operation associated with any of these issues, like poor time management or self-control, the typical response is to engage in horizontal development. We think, either for ourselves or others, that we or they need better skills for time management or self-control. But Russell Barkley says that for those with ADHD, not learning these things is "not a matter of 'won't' but of 'can't.'" This is because these are not Doing Side deficiencies, they are Being Side deficiencies that are directly tied to the three executive processing networks introduced in the last chapter: the salience network, default mode network, and central executive network.

About these networks, Vinod Menon, a neuroscientist at Stanford University, wrote: "These three brain networks come up over and over in pretty much every cognitive task we ask subjects to do. They are critical for information processing and attending to stimuli in the environment." What Menon and his colleagues have found is that people with ADHD have weaker interactions between these networks than people who do not have it, a difference that is easily distinguishable via fMRI brain scans.

So, while trauma seems to cause either the salience network or the default mode network to become overactive, ADHD is a neurological condition where the three brain networks are less functionally connected. Both of these programming issues serve to impede one's internal operating system from operating at a high Being Side altitude.

Before we move on, there are several other aspects to know about ADHD as it relates to our Being Side.

Additional Insights Associated with ADHD

First, ADHD researchers have found that the condition's neurological deficiencies are mostly genetic, or caused by nature. This is different than the neurological deficiencies associated with trauma, which are largely caused by nurture. But researchers have also found that people with ADHD are more prone to experience trauma. In fact, there is evidence that children with ADHD are four times more likely to develop post-traumatic stress disorder. ADHD researchers surmise that this relationship exists because children with ADHD have more behavioral issues, making them more susceptible to violence or abuse and putting themselves in harm's way, and are less likely to receive the care and support they need after a traumatic experience.

Second, medical professionals generally acknowledge that the symptoms of ADHD generally show up in three different ways, leading to the identification of three different types of ADHD: ADHD-Inattentive, ADHD-Hyperactive, and ADHD-Combined. People with ADHD-Inattentive primarily struggle with attention and concentration. They have trouble sustaining and regulating attention, organizing tasks, and following instructions, and they have a lower processing speed. People with ADHD-Hyperactive are more hyperactive and restless, often interrupting others and acting impulsively without considering consequences. And people with ADHD-Combined experience a combination of all these symptoms.

Third, childhood ADHD generally does not go away as one transitions into adulthood. But one's relationship with the condition is likely to change as they age. It is not uncommon for people with childhood ADHD to develop skills to manage it, for their ADHD to manifest differently, or for one's symptoms to reduce.

Fourth, males are more likely to experience ADHD-Hyperactive, while females more often experience ADHD-Inattentive. Further, ADHD-Inattentive is more likely to go undiagnosed. A big reason for this is because if one struggles with hyperactivity, restlessness,

It has been estimated
that up to 75 percent of
adults who have ADHD
are undiagnosed.

———————————

or impulse control, it is quite physically obvious. As a result, people with ADHD-Hyperactive are more likely to seek out diagnosis and support. But if one struggles with attention regulation, task organization, and lower processing speed, it is not as apparent. This means that ADHD researchers are finding that there are a lot of adult women who struggle with ADHD-Inattentive and do not realize they have it. As a whole, 10 percent of children have received a formal diagnosis of ADHD. While this suggests that roughly 10 percent of people likely have the condition, the real percentage is probably higher because it has been estimated that up to 75 percent of adults who have it are undiagnosed. In fact, most women with ADHD do not get an accurate diagnosis of their ADHD until their late 30s or 40s, a finding that holds true with my wife.

Back to My Family

At the beginning of this chapter, I explained how my daughter's ADHD diagnosis led to me learning more about the condition and investigating its connection to our internal operating system. This diagnosis, and our learning about ADHD, also led my wife to wonder if she and our son had it. We decided to get both of them tested.

Sure enough, both have ADHD, specifically ADHD-Combined. While my wife and two children all have ADHD-Combined, we find it interesting that each of them manifests quite different symptoms. My son does not struggle with restlessness, but he does have a racing mind. My daughter has difficulty with time management. And my wife tends to struggle with the consequences of diminished working memory.

In chapter 6, you read about how this diagnosis was eye-opening and helpful for my wife. She was able to seek out treatment via neurofeedback therapy to address the neurological deficiencies associated with her ADHD. This effort proved to be much more fruitful for her than the trauma therapy that she engaged in.

It has also been helpful to know that our children have ADHD. Now knowing more about ADHD, we have come to realize that we weren't always providing the best support and environment for children with the condition. But now we are doing a better job of providing a good environment, access to helpful support in their schooling, and access to neurofeedback therapy to directly address the neurological deficiencies that come with ADHD. I'll share more about neurofeedback therapy in the coming chapters as we discuss how we can go about upgrading our internal operating system to *become better*.

Key Discoveries

Across my family's experience with trauma and ADHD, one primary lesson has stood out to me, which is part of the reason I feel so compelled to write this book. It is this: There are a lot of people out there who have neurological deficiencies, whether the result of trauma, ADHD, or something else. Whatever those deficiencies are the result of, they are holding us back from being our best selves. I recognize that some people's neurological deficiencies prevent them from upgrading their internal operating system. But they are rare. There are so many people who are either like me (someone who has neurodeficiencies because of past trauma), my wife (who has neurodeficiencies as a result of ADHD), or a combination of the two of us, whose neurodeficiencies can be overcome. And, to the degree that we overcome them, we get closer to becoming our ideal selves. In fact, if we want to *become better*, we will need to overcome them. That is why vertical development is so critical. Horizontal development does not address neurodeficiencies. Until those are addressed, the wiring of our internal operating system will continue to be an impediment to our goals and aspirations.

We are now ready to move on to the third step of the *becoming better* journey, the step where the rubber meets the road. You should feel like you have gotten clarity on what your Being Side is (step #1) and have a greater awareness of your Being Side altitude (step #2). Next, we'll explore how we implement vertical development to upgrade our internal operating system so that we elevate along our Being Side and *become better* (step #3).

Applications for Leadership

Imagine if you have a leader with ADHD who struggles with things like self-awareness, inhibition, working memory, time management, emotional self-control, self-motivation, or self-organization. This does not mean that the leader is not capable of doing great things, but it's pretty obvious that they have room to *become better*. And if the leader can get the appropriate development and support to address deficiencies associated with ADHD, they will be able to create greater value.

If, as you read this chapter, you saw aspects of yourself in the signals of ADHD, I encourage you to get tested for it so that you can get the support you need. While you can do a great job as a leader even if you have ADHD, your ability to elevate as a leader will be limited if you do not take steps to improve your neurofunctionality. From my experience working with business leaders, it is my hunch that at least 10 percent of leaders have ADHD, most of whom are unaware that they have it.

Also, if you have reason to believe that there are leaders or employees in your organization that have ADHD, could you provide them with access to testing and support?

My family wishes we would have known about ADHD earlier, because it is only when we had this awareness that we became more supportive, more impactful, and more value-creating.

PART THREE

To Become Better, You Must Elevate Along Your Being Side

16

The Difference Between Horizontal and Vertical Development

Becoming isn't about arriving somewhere or achieving a certain aim. I see it instead as forward motion, a means of evolving, a way to reach continuously toward a better self. The journey doesn't end.

MICHELLE OBAMA

N HER BOOK *Rising Strong*, Brené Brown uses a term to describe a necessary condition of elevating along our Being Side. The term is "rumble." Whenever I think of the word, in my mind I hear Michael Buffer, the world-renowned boxing and wrestling ring announcer who would start bouts with his famous catchphrase, "Let's get ready to rumble!"

I think the notion of "rumble" in the context of boxing or wrestling is fitting for what is required to vertically develop and elevate along our Being Side. You may not like to hear that, but it is a necessary part of vertical development. If you want to *become better*, you are going to have to do some rumbling.

From Brené's experience elevating along her Being Side, she writes that to rise strong, or elevate, we have to be willing to rumble with our stories. By "rumble" she means that we have to "get honest about the stories [we've] made up... Rumbling with our story and owning our truth in order to write a new, more courageous ending transforms who we are and how we engage with the world... The rumble is where wholeheartedness is cultivated and change begins."

Over the next couple of chapters, we are going to explore specific ways that we may need to rumble in order to *become better*. But first, let's prepare for the rumbling by covering some key distinctions between horizontal and vertical development.

The Key Emphasis and Activities of Horizontal Development

When we engage in horizontal development, the primary emphasis is on improving our skills. This generally involves three basic activities. The first is becoming *aware* of our skill gaps. Then, once we are clear on our gaps, the next activity is *practicing* the skill we are trying to develop to close them. The third activity is getting *coaching* or guidance. Generally, the more coaching we receive, the more quickly we close the skill gap we are working on.

Let's bring horizontal development to life with a couple of examples.

First, when I was a high school basketball player, I wanted to improve my shooting ability. I was aware that I was a good shooter, but not yet great. So I not only practiced a lot, but every year our coach brought in the original "shot doctor" coach, Ernie Hobbie, to train us on our shooting form and technique. With his help, I was able to learn the mechanics and fundamentals of shooting that I would have never learned otherwise, speeding up my improvement as a shooter.

HORIZONTAL DEVELOPMENT Emphasis: Improving skills	
Developmental Efforts	**Focus of Efforts**
1. Awareness	Skill gaps
2. Practice	Skill development
3. Coaching	Direction for improving skills

VERTICAL DEVELOPMENT Emphasis: Upgrading our internal operating system	
Developmental Efforts	**Focus of Efforts**
1. Awareness	Neural programming
2. Practice	Try out new neural pathways
3. Coaching	Guidance for 1 and 2
4. Improved Neurology	Rewire the mind

As another example, let's explore a pet peeve of mine: how most emotional intelligence gurus go about helping people increase their emotional intelligence. They have yet to understand that one's capacity for emotional intelligence is a Being Side ability determined by the quality and sophistication of our internal operating system. Thus, these gurus treat emotional intelligence as a Doing Side skill and implement horizontal development programming that focuses primarily on developing certain skills associated with emotional intelligence.

The skills that are most commonly focused on in these emotional intelligence programs are how to listen more effectively, practice empathy, and have crucial conversations. Thus, the programs generally involve (1) efforts to help people become more aware of their emotional intelligence deficiencies or gaps in these areas; (2)

role-playing to practice the skills of listening, being empathetic, and having crucial conversations; and (3) receiving coaching to help speed up the skill development process.

The reason this is a pet peeve for me is not because this approach can't be beneficial; it can. I just find that it is shortsighted because it fails to appreciate the fact that while one may have the knowledge and skills related to how to listen, practice empathy, or have crucial conversations, being able to effectively put them to use in the "heat of the moment" is contingent upon the quality of a person's internal operating system.

Thus, if we want people to make transformational progress in their emotional intelligence, we need a different form of development focused on upgrading their internal operating system. Hence, vertical development.

The Key Emphasis and Activities of Vertical Development

When we engage in vertical development, the primary emphasis is not on improving our skills but on upgrading our internal operating system. And while the three activities involved in horizontal development are used in vertical development, their focus is dramatically different. Additionally, there is a fourth activity necessary for vertical development that is not a part of horizontal development.

First, *awareness* in the context of vertical development is focused on our neural programming. Individuals are invited to explore the quality and sophistication of their automatic and nonconscious programming. They can do this by learning about their vertical development altitude, the quality of their mindsets, and their *if-then* programming.

Second, *practice* in the context of vertical development is focused on experimenting with alternative and more value-creating ways of

When we engage in vertical development, the primary emphasis is not on improving our skills, but on upgrading our internal operating system.

---

operating that differ from our normal neural programming. Let me give you several examples from a few different perspectives. If I am in Mind 1.0 and I am reluctant to take charge of something because I am wired to stay safe, comfortable, and feel like I fit in, I may want to experiment with taking charge of something small as a way to push against my fears and insecurities. If I have more of a fixed mindset that makes it difficult for me to step into learning zone challenges, I may want to take on a challenge that will help me learn and grow. For me, since I have *if-then* programming where *if* my children start fighting with each other, *then* I quickly lose patience, I may want to experiment with being intentional about staying positive and within my window of tolerance when my children fight.

Third, when it comes to *coaching*, my opinion is that for horizontal development, it is a "nice-to-have." While it can speed up horizontal development, I do not think it is absolutely needed. But coaching for vertical development, I believe, is much more of a "need-to-have." After years of doing vertical development work with leaders and others, I have learned that it is very difficult for someone to (1) become adequately aware of their neural programming and (2) step into the discomfort of practicing and experimenting with new and more value-creating neural programming without the assistance of a coach. For people to do this work successfully and to the depth that is generally required, they need a personal development or business coach familiar with vertical development. That coach can be a mindset coach, business coach, therapist, or psychiatrist. As we go through part 3, I'll try my best to serve as your coach on these things, and also provide you with additional resources.

Fourth, the activity that is unique to vertical development is engaging in efforts to *improve our neurology*. Vertical development requires that we literally alter and improve the neural connections in our mind and body. In the coming chapters, I will go into depth on various tactics designed to improve our neurology. But for now,

I'll provide a relatively basic example of such an effort: meditation. Research on meditation has found that it helps to modulate the neural connectivity between our default mode network, salience network, and central executive network, and thus improves our capabilities related to attention, executive function, and emotional regulation.

Often, the efforts to improve our neurology are like meditation. They are small but frequent interventions. The reason is because our neural connections are a lot like our muscles—the more we use them, the stronger we become. We will never become strong by working out once; we must work out again and again and again. The same thing goes for improving our neural connections. We have to develop habits and practices to regularly exercise our brain.

Key Discoveries

By comparing and contrasting the emphasis and efforts of horizontal and vertical development, I hope you have gotten the sense that vertical development might be quite different than the traditional horizontal development processes you have engaged with in the past. And, I'll be honest, vertical development efforts are uncomfortable. They have to be by their very nature. These efforts require us to activate and utilize neural connection pathways that we are not used to using. We are going to have to push back on our typical processing habits.

But one of the keys to doing this successfully is to avoid pushing too hard, too soon. This understanding has shaped the strategy of the next three chapters, which are focused on helping you engage in vertical development to transformationally *become better*.

- Chapter 17 is going to focus on starter-level vertical development strategies and activities. These are ideal for those just starting on their vertical development journey.

- In chapter 18, we will move into deeper vertical development strategies and activities associated with upgrading our mindsets.

- Then, in chapter 19, we will shift into even deeper vertical development strategies and activities that focus on healing from trauma and working through neurodeficiencies associated with ADHD. Such efforts generally take working with a trained and certified professional.

As you go through these chapters, I challenge you to select different activities that involve the four vertical development efforts identified in this chapter: deepening your awareness of your current programming, practicing or trying out new neural pathways, getting the assistance of a coach, and upgrading your neurology.

Let's jump in so that you can start elevating!

Applications for Leadership

I mentioned this previously, but it is an idea worth repeating: Leaders' Being Side altitude sets the ceiling for the effectiveness and success of the groups they lead.

So if you are a leader, as we go into these final chapters, ask yourself: What vertical development efforts am I going to engage in to elevate my altitude so that I can elevate my team and my organization?

And, if you are someone who helps leaders to develop, ask yourself: What activities, practices, and resources do I need to introduce to my leaders to help them elevate their altitude?

17

Starter-Level Activities to Elevate Your Being Side

Don't let who you were talk you out of who you are becoming.
BOB GOFF

SOMEONE WHO HAS HARNESSED vertical development to radically transform and elevate himself is David Goggins. He went from an abused and neglected child to a washed-out Air Force veteran to a 300-plus-pound night exterminator to a Navy SEAL after having to go through Hell Week three times, and finally an ultra-endurance athlete. In his *New York Times* best-selling 2018 autobiography, *Can't Hurt Me,* David shares his transformational journey, along with great tips and tactics he learned and employed to climb the vertical development ladder, one step at a time. In this chapter, we'll leverage his journey and his recommended practices to help you get a sense of ways that you can start climbing the ladder too. While I believe that David Goggins is a great example of someone who has leveraged vertical development practices to transformationally become better, if you know of him, you also know he can be extreme and abrasive. So, let's also keep in mind that he is someone who is still climbing the vertical development mountain, which is also featured in his subsequent book, *Never Finished*.

David Goggins's Vertical Development Journey

According to his autobiography, David Goggins's life started rough. From an early age, his father, Trunnis Goggins, forced him, his brother, and his mother into working at his skating rink, with little personal benefit to themselves. They had to work late, sleeping on a couch in a back room until his dad closed up for the night. And the couch David slept on had a gun tucked under the seat cushion, a gun that would be used as a threat against David, his brother, and his mom. But Trunnis did more than just threaten. Trunnis frequently beat and withheld necessary healthcare from David, his brother, and especially his wife.

When David was around six years old, he recalls his mom wanting to give him a bright spot in his life. So, she signed him up for Cub Scouts. He was so excited. He still remembers putting on the navy blue, button-down Cub Scout shirt. He wrote, "I felt proud wearing a uniform and knowing at least for a few hours I could pretend to be a normal kid." Just as they were heading out the door, his father came home and glared at him. And rather than let him go to Cub Scouts, his father took him to the horse racing track for a day of betting. At the end of the day, his father had lost thousands of dollars and wouldn't shut up about it on the drive home. David glared at him from the rear seat. Seeing this in his rearview mirror, his father asked, "You got something to say?!"

Still bummed about not going to Cub Scouts, David responded, "We shouldn't have gone to the track anyway," which led to Trunnis blowing his top. His dad tried to smack him from the driver's seat, which David was able to avoid. Catching his breath, his dad said,

"When we get home, you're gonna take your clothes off," meaning that he was ready to bestow a serious beatdown.

Getting home, he stripped down and lay over his parents' bed, butt exposed. His dad then proceeded to whip him with his belt all down his back, butt, and legs. This left him in a state where he couldn't go to school for several days.

After a couple of more years of enduring this abuse, when David was in second grade his mom, in extreme fear and uncertainty, took the two boys, left Trunnis, and drove to her parents' home in Brazil, Indiana.

In Brazil, David was put in school, where it quickly became clear that he was well behind his peers. He was labeled as "special" and was the only black kid in class. Between the chaos and abuse that he had lived through, the stress of moving to a new place, and being singled out in negative ways at school, the stress began taking its toll. He developed a stutter, his hair started falling out, and white blotches bloomed on his dark skin.

Brazil, Indiana, is only an hour's drive from a former Ku Klux Klan hotspot, and throughout his upbringing there he experienced racist bullying and threats, including at one point having a gun put to his head.

Given what he had been through, it shouldn't come as a surprise that he had some behavioral issues during high school. Despite basketball being his love and something he worked tirelessly at, he was cut from the basketball team his junior year. This had less to do with his ability and more to do with his attitude and that he didn't go to the team's offseason workouts.

Around this same time, his mom kicked him out of the house because he came home from a party after curfew. Of this, he wrote in *Can't Hurt Me*, "In my mind, I had already been living by myself for several years. I made my own meals, cleaned my own clothes. I wasn't angry at her. I was cocky and I figured I didn't need her anymore." He stayed at friends' houses for the next 10 days. At that point his mom called him at his friend's house to tell him that she got a letter from the school saying he had missed over a quarter of the year due to unexcused absences, had a D average, and was not on track to graduate. He came home and read the letter.

It was then that he decided his life needed to change. And it was here that he would take his first big step upward in becoming better. In his words:

> That night, after taking a shower, I wiped the steam away from our corroded bathroom mirror and took a good look. I didn't like who I saw staring back. I was a low-budget thug with no purpose and no future. I felt so disgusted I wanted to punch [myself] in the face and shatter glass. Instead, I lectured him. It was time to get real.

While lecturing himself, he reached for the shaving cream and started shaving the peach fuzz on his cheeks and ultimately his scalp, desperate for a change and to become someone new.

Of this experience, which would prove to be transformative, he recalls,

> A new ritual was born, one that stayed with me for years. It would help me get my grades up, whip my sorry ass into shape, and see me through graduation and into the Air Force. The ritual was simple. I'd shave ... every night, get loud, and get real. I set goals, wrote them on Post-It notes, and tagged them to what I now call the Accountability Mirror, because each day I'd hold myself accountable to the goals I'd set.

In my opinion, this daily practice definitely didn't improve his talent, knowledge, skills, or abilities, but it did help him elevate along his Being Side, which was transformational. He started to see himself less as a victim and began to take ownership of his life. By doing the little things to elevate his internal operating system, he started to operate in very different and more elevated ways. He threw away his baggy clothes and started tucking in his shirt. He stopped eating at his friends' lunch table and ate alone. He started working out at 5 a.m. and ran all the time.

This was just the start of David Goggins's personal transformation. Through some ups and downs and a lot of vertical development work, he eventually went on to become not only a Navy SEAL and ultra-endurance athlete, but also a smoke jumper and wildland firefighter. If you want the details of his incredible journey, I highly recommend reading his two books, *Can't Hurt Me* and *Never Finished*.

The Starter-Level Strategies for Becoming Better

One of the reasons I have leveraged David Goggins as a focal example in this chapter is because I had initially written a list of as many starter-level vertical development practices that I could identify, and when I reread David's books, I saw that he engaged in almost all of them!

As I introduce these practices to you, recognize that they do not involve big or significant efforts. They are about engaging in small, relatively insignificant practices repeatedly over time. The reason why they work is because they are designed to upgrade the wiring of our internal operating system.

It is important for us to realize that our minds, like most new cars, have a self-protective governor that holds us back from operating at our highest level in an effort to stay safe, comfortable, and not burn too hot. A lesson that anyone who has vertically developed themselves has learned is that to vertically develop, we need to intentionally break through our governor settings. We need to realize that our programming and default settings may have done a good job of getting us where we are today, but they are unlikely to get us to a higher-level version of ourselves.

We need to realize that our programming and default settings may have done a good job of getting us where we are today, but they are unlikely to get us to a higher-level version of ourselves.

———————————————

To help his readers understand this, David introduces what he calls the "40 Percent Rule." Through his efforts to push against his own personal governor, he has learned that when we think we have given our maximum effort, we have only given 40 percent of what we can possibly give.

The following practices are great starter-level activities to engage in to push against your governor, upgrade your internal wiring and programming, and step into a more elevated version of yourself.

The Accountability Mirror

As mentioned, the first step of David Goggins's *becoming better* journey was the use of his "accountability mirror." What made this powerful for David was that it helped him do three things on a daily basis. First, he regularly connected with his goals and aspirations. Second, he evaluated the degree to which he was moving in the direction of those ambitions. And third, he used the practice of daily self-talk to activate and strengthen his value-creating mindset's neural connections. These are all small but mighty activities that can help upgrade our internal operating system.

David writes, "It was the Accountability Mirror that kept me motivated to keep pushing toward something better." He harnessed the power of the Accountability Mirror to change his lifestyle, change his look, change his friends, work out relentlessly, study hard, get his grades up, and pass the aptitude test for entrance into the Air Force. The mirror helped him live with purpose, and that changed everything for him.

While he would ebb and flow with this practice, he continually came back to the Accountability Mirror when he recognized a need to step up in his *becoming better* journey. It is a practice he encourages his readers and listeners to engage in regularly.

Interestingly, before I read *Can't Hurt Me*, I had created my own Accountability Wall. I didn't call it that, but that is what it was. After I got fired from my consulting job at Gallup and returned to being a professor at Cal State Fullerton, I felt like I was nowhere near where I wanted to be in life. And I realized that the only person who could create the life I wanted was me. So, I put my biggest long-term goals on Post-It notes at the top of my wall. Then, below those, I created layers of sticky notes identifying the different steps that I would need to take to eventually reach the top-level goals, and connected those steps with string. In the end, my wall almost looked like a spider web. I had five or six rows of steps that I had to climb, which included starting my own business, writing a book, writing multiple books, establishing an online platform and presence, engaging in research, and getting tenure, among others. While this felt a bit daunting, I had my paths laid out for creating the life I dreamed of. I just needed to focus on taking the first steps along the bottom.

At the time I created my Accountability Wall, I figured it would take me at least 10 years to accomplish everything on it. Fast-forwarding six years, when we moved out of our house I had to take the Accountability Wall down. It was an emotional moment for me as I basked in the realization that I had been able to climb from the lower-level goals to the higher-level goals, accomplishing all of them in less than six years.

This stuff works!

But the Accountability Mirror isn't the only starter-level vertical development practice that we can engage in. In what follows, I'll share six other research-backed practices for upgrading our internal operating system, some of which David Goggins also harnessed as part of his vertical development journey.

Journaling

Journaling is effective for vertical development because it forces us to activate and stimulate more value-creating neural connections.

When I was first invited to journal, I was incredibly resistant, thinking "there is no way I am going to journal." But figuring that it wasn't going to hurt to try, I gave myself two weeks to test-drive journaling, using a notebook called *The Five Minute Journal*. I told myself that if journaling in this book doesn't add any value to my life after two weeks, I would toss it in the trash. I have now been using *The Five Minute Journal* for over seven years because I have found it so beneficial for helping me get in and stay in value-creation mode.

Through my practice and studying other journaling practices, I have learned that there are a few different ways we can leverage journaling to facilitate vertical development.

The first way is to journal about all of the factors that are limiting or have limited your growth and success. This allows us to use our story, our challenges, and our setbacks to fuel our ultimate success. David Goggins primarily used this journaling approach to help him take inventory of his life, own his past, and rise above it.

A second way to journal is to write down your achievement hit list. Journal about the obstacles you've overcome. Journal about the times when you never gave up, when you persevered and ultimately succeeded. Write about the feelings that came with succeeding, overcoming your struggles, and winning. This practice helps us remember that we have risen above challenges before and can rise above the challenges ahead.

A third way to journal is to write about your most heart-wrenching failures and conduct your own after-action report. This includes writing about and evaluating your process and your mindsets along the way. Identify where you fell short, what you learned, and what you can fix. Be brutally honest with yourself. Then, close out your journaling by writing about how you have benefited from your failure and what you are going to do moving forward. This is a great practice for activating and strengthening your growth mindset's neural connections.

There is no one right way to journal. What is most important to recognize is that just by going through the motions of putting pen to paper or fingers to keyboard, it forces us to activate and stimulate different and new neurological patterns and mindset neural connections. Yes, you can think through these different practices and that will be helpful, but your brain will benefit more from going through the process of writing.

Record Yourself

This is another way to leverage the power of self-talk. Throughout his adult life, David Goggins has recorded himself and used listening to those recordings to help him rise above his challenges. In his book *Never Finished*, he reports that while journaling has been helpful, recording himself has had a more profound impact on his mind and life. David has found success using this practice in several different ways. Sometimes he records himself complaining and plays it back, which allows him to better catch the flaws in his thinking. Other times, he'll record himself reciting criticisms that have been made about him. He listens to this criticism to motivate himself to reach new heights. And he has also found it healing to record himself reciting his fears, traumas, and abuse, which helps him neutralize the painful stories he has had to carry, helping him to heal. For him, this has brought transformational energy to help him change and elevate his life.

For me, I have also found huge value retelling my fears and traumas. Through my therapy journey, I learned that if I can voice my fears and verbally surface the pain from my trauma, the weight of those fears and traumas diminishes.

Meditation

There is a wide variety of types of meditations and ways to meditate.

At its core, meditation is a scientifically validated exercise for your brain that involves focusing on and connecting to your breathing and your body. And because you are human, as you meditate your mind will inevitably wander away from your breath and body. That is okay, it is a part of meditating. The key to meditation is being able to recognize that your mind has wandered and bringing your attention and focus back to your breath and body. Dan Harris, the author of *10% Happier*, states that every time our mind races off and we rein it in and connect back to our breath and body, that is like a bicep curl for our brain. Of course, over time the idea is to expand our ability to stay present and aware of our breath and body for longer and longer.

Research has found that meditation regulates our nervous system. Specifically, it deactivates our sympathetic nervous system, the part of our nervous system responsible for our fight-or-flight responses, and it activates our parasympathetic nervous system, the part responsible for our body's ability to relax. Regular meditation serves to widen our window of tolerance and make us less prone to lose control of our emotions and cognitions in the heat of the moment, allowing us to stay more present and in touch with ourselves when stressed.

At the brain level, meditation improves and strengthens the interconnection between our default mode and salience networks. When this connection is strengthened, we are able to better regulate ourselves, encode our world in more accurate and value-creating ways, and operate with higher levels of emotional intelligence.

I used to see meditation as some sort of hippie practice. But now it is an important part of my *becoming better* efforts. Every morning, I meditate using a free meditation app called Insight Timer.

Yoga

Yoga is a practice that combines body movements, breath control, and meditation. Research is finding that yoga has the same effects on our nervous system and mind as meditation. Thus, it is another activity that helps us *become better*. You can join a class, where you may also get a sense of community that inspires you to keep going, or if you're shy there are plenty of free videos for beginners online. It's also a great activity you can do with kids, making the whole household calmer and more present. We've used yoga to help our children wind down before going to bed.

Gratitude Journaling

Gratitude journaling is a practice that involves regularly writing down the things that you are grateful for. While this surely helps us feel happier, research is finding that this practice has deeper-level benefits. Like with meditation, gratitude journaling activates our parasympathetic nervous system, which helps reduce our stress in the moment. And, over time, this practice helps improve our body's stress-carrying capacity. At the brain level, researchers have found that gratitude improves the functioning of our default mode network and salience network in such a way that it alleviates pain, improves interpersonal relationships, and increases our willingness to engage in prosocial behaviors.

Cold Plunges

Cold plunges, also known as cold therapy, involves immersing one's body in cold water for a short period of time. This has almost the opposite effect on our nervous system to meditation and yoga in that it activates our sympathetic nervous system. It shocks our fight-or-flight response. The idea of purposely doing this is to, over time, enhance our body's ability to tolerate stress and build resistance. When we intentionally shock our body's nervous system via cold water immersion, it helps us develop the capacity to better regulate ourselves when we find ourselves in stressful situations. And while research on how cold plunges affect our brain is limited, there is initial evidence that they strengthen the connection between the default mode network and the salience network.

Key Discoveries

After you've worked through this chapter and the various start-er-level strategies, I hope that three lessons stand out to you:

1   Vertical development practices are quite different than the typical horizontal development efforts that we engage in.

2   Vertical development practices are designed to upgrade the programming of our internal operating system.

3   Vertical development practices require that we develop habits and routines around doing "the little things." We have got to be focused and intentional about engaging in these efforts.

Of these points, David Goggins says, "Everything in life is about repetition... Reps. You have to put the repetition in. A lot of people, they do something once and they give up on it. This is something that you have to do every day of your life... It can't be something that you do every now and again."

From a neuroscience standpoint, we know this is true. The way we *become better* is by upgrading our internal operating system, by improving the functionality of our body's nervous system. And this requires reps.

Effectively, if we want to vertically develop, we *have* to hit the gym for our brain. When we go to a gym to work out, there are maybe 100 different machines that we can use. When it comes to vertical development, what matters less is which exercise or workout you do. What matters more is that you are there in the gym working out. So, choose whichever of these workouts you want to do, and put in the reps.

For now, identify at least one of the above exercises that you can engage in on a regular basis and start practicing. For me, I have found value in leveraging James Clear's advice in his book *Atomic*

Habits to habit stack. Habit stacking is taking a current habit or routine that you have and adding an activity to that. For me, every morning I habit stack my journaling and meditation together as the first thing I do when I sit down in my office.

Applications for Leadership

Being in a leadership position is incredibly demanding physically, emotionally, relationally, and spiritually. To operate at a high level, leaders need to continually replenish their tank or battery. It is difficult to lead from a Mind 3.0 level without that energy.

While most leaders understand this, my experience working with executives is that a very small percentage of them are actually engaging in activities designed to add positivity and energy to their tank, activities like the ones I have identified in this chapter. Most executives say they are too busy or don't have the time. To me, this is a signal of an underdeveloped internal operating system that is wired more to be concerned about urgent, short-term needs, which is causing them to underappreciate and underinvest in more important, long-term needs, like replenishing their tank every day.

So if you are a leader and are not engaging in at least some of the practices in this chapter on a daily basis, while you may be trying really hard to be a good leader, I imagine that you are underperforming. See if you can make some habit changes with this book as your guide.

18

Deeper-Level Activities to Elevate Your Being Side

Life is about being and becoming, not having and getting.
STEPHANIE SEABROOK HEDGEPATH

F WE WANT to take our vertical development efforts to a deeper level, we need to focus on our mindsets and develop a plan for elevating them.

In this chapter, I will discuss why focusing on mindsets is a deep, powerful, and ideal way to vertically develop along our Being Side, and how to go about doing so.

The Power of Mindsets for Elevating Along Your Being Side

A couple of years ago, I was doing a series of four workshops on mindsets with an executive team. The first three workshops were virtual, and the last one was a half-day session in person. After doing the first three workshops, I was a little concerned about one of the executive team members. I'll call him Max.

I was concerned about Max because during the first three sessions he never spoke up or engaged with the group. And, I'll be honest, he looked a little intimidating. Being on Zoom, I could only see him from his shoulders up. But I think the best way to describe what I saw was that he looked like someone who owned a Harley-Davidson motorcycle: he was a big guy, he had a full beard, and he never showed anything but a stoic, "don't mess with me" face. By the time it came for me to meet with the team in person, I was questioning whether he was buying into the leadership and mindset concepts I was promoting to the group.

As I drove over to the company's office on the morning of our final and in-person session, I considered the social dynamics I was facing. For me, Max was a bit of a wild card. In my mind, the worst-case scenario was that he wouldn't buy into the ideas I would be promoting and would become a vocal disruptor. I didn't know what to expect.

But any anxiety related to Max that I felt went away as we started the session because Max wasn't there.

About 10 minutes in and feeling on a roll, I noticed everyone's heads turn toward the doorway at my back. As I followed suit, I was caught off guard because there was Max. What surprised me was not simply that it was Max, it was how big he was. Max filled the door. At probably six feet, seven inches tall and likely weighing about 300 pounds of what appeared to be solid muscle, he was a commanding and unavoidable presence. Recognizing that he was a bit of a distraction, he quietly took a seat, and we proceeded with the session.

Now seeing Max in person, he remained a bit of a mystery and still a potential wild card. So during our first break, I decided to check in with him. I wanted to get to know him and see how he was feeling about the content I was presenting. Trying to be as friendly as possible, I greeted him with a bit of small talk before I got to a question that I was burning to ask. I said, "During our virtual sessions, I am not sure I remember you making any comments. So I am curious, how is this material sitting with you?"

Given his appearance and stature, I was expecting a "tough guy" answer that was dismissive. But in the moments after I asked the question, he averted his eyes and seemed to grow solemn. When he looked back at me, he said the thing I least expected. In a serious tone, he said, "This stuff has changed my life."

Caught off guard by this response, I probed: "Tell me more."

Max went on to explain that before I started working with the team, he had never given any thought to his mindsets. But after presenting him with my mindset framework and having him take my mindset assessment, he said he now thinks and is intentional about his mindsets every day. He went so far as to say, "You can even ask my wife, and she will tell you that I am a changed man."

Expounding further, Max said the mindset set that had been the most helpful for him to get in touch with was the closed and open mindsets. His mindset assessment revealed that he had a strong closed mindset, and after learning about what a closed mindset was and how it can be limiting, he started to see how it was protecting him in some ways (e.g., helping him feel in control) but was also hindering his relationships with his wife and children. After awakening to his closed mindset, he started working on adopting more of an open one. And it was this shift that helped him to become a different and improved person.

This was music to my ears. I love hearing stories like this. And fortunately, I get to hear them quite often, because that is the power of mindsets. When we can help people awaken to them, we give them the opportunity to improve their mindsets. And as people improve their mindsets, they *become better*.

When we can help people
awaken to their mindsets, we give
them the opportunity to improve their
mindsets. And, as people improve
their mindsets, they *become better*.

———————————

Why Focusing on Mindsets is Critical to Vertical Development

Why is it that focusing on mindsets can have this life-elevating impact?

Let me answer this question at two different levels of depth.

For the first, more surface-level answer, we need to go back to our definition of vertical development. At its core, vertical development involves enhancing our ability to make meaning of our world in more cognitively and emotionally sophisticated ways. Well, what are our "meaning makers?" Our meaning makers are our mindsets. So, when we focus on improving our mindsets, we are directly focusing on our vertical development.

For the second, deeper-level answer, we need to connect back to the neuroscience of our internal operating system. Remember that our mindsets play three foundational roles in our operating system: First, they play the role of our mental filter, filtering only the information they deem relevant into our brain; second, they interpret that information in unique ways, generally either more self-protective or value-creating; and third, they activate our body's response to this information based on how it is interpreted. And on top of this, our mindsets generally perform these roles below the level of our consciousness.

What I have learned is that if we can become conscious of our mindsets and the default manner that our internal operating system is wired to process our world, we give ourselves the opportunity to reprogram and upgrade our operating system. That is what happened with Max. He awakened to his mindsets. After becoming conscious of them, he engaged in efforts to alter and improve how he made meaning of his world. And by doing so, he upgraded how he is programmed to think and operate. As a result, he has *become better*.

There is no getting around it: if you are going to elevate along your Being Side, you are going to have to elevate and improve how you make meaning of your world. This means that you are going to have to elevate and improve your mindsets.

Now, the starter-level strategies in chapter 17 are things that you can do to elevate and improve your mindsets. But they do not necessarily involve a direct focus on your mindsets. We can speed up our *becoming better* journey by focusing directly on mindsets, and I hope the example of Max helped you to see that.

From my experience, people are most successful at upgrading their mindsets when they identify a specific one they want to focus on, and then develop a plan to elevate it. So, as we move into the next section of this chapter, I want you to pick one of the mindsets that you want to improve: growth, open, promotion, or outward. Because next, I will help you craft a personal mindset development plan focused on it.

Creating a Personal Mindset Development Plan

Okay, which mindset do you want to develop more? Is it a growth, open, promotion, or outward mindset?

With the value-creating mindset in mind, let me ask you two questions. First, do you think that developing this mindset will be easy or difficult?

Most people think "difficult."

Second, do you think that developing this mindset is more about doing big, heavy, infrequent activities or more about doing small, lighter, more frequent ones?

Not that big, heavy, infrequent activities won't help, but the reality is that we shift our mindsets via small, light, and frequent activities. It is about doing the work of rewiring our neurology, which takes repetition.

From this perspective, I am never going to say that shifting our mindsets is easy, but I do believe it is easier than we generally think.

To help you embrace this idea, let me remind you that our mindsets are neural connections. This is important to recognize because our neural connections are a lot like our muscles: the more we use them, the stronger they become. So, if we want to adopt more value-creating mindsets, we need to continually exercise and strengthen our value-creating mindset neural connections. This takes small, light, and frequent activities more than it does big, heavy, infrequent activities.

In fact, I find it helpful to think about the process of shifting our mindsets as being similar to learning how to count to 10 in a different language. It requires three steps.

The first step to learning how to count to 10 in a different language is to have the motivation to do so and believe it is possible. Hopefully you now have the motivation to work on your mindset, and you are trusting me enough to believe that shifting your mindset is possible.

The second step is to learn the words associated with the numbers. So, if I want to learn how to count to 10 in Spanish, I need to learn that *uno* means one, *dos* means two, *tres* means three, etc. In a similar fashion, we need to put labels to mindsets. We have done that in this book. I have helped you learn about four different sets of mindsets and how they differ from each other. You now have the labels of fixed and growth, closed and open, prevention and promotion, and inward and outward. The power of having these labels is that it allows you to shine a light on what they represent. Before reading this book, if you didn't know about these mindset labels, it is likely that your mindsets existed in the dark, below the level of your consciousness. But now, by shedding light on them, you have the ability to look at and evaluate your mindsets. You have come a long way in learning the language of mindsets.

The third step is to actually do the work of practicing counting to 10 in that language. This does not require big, grand efforts. It simply requires practicing five to 10 minutes a day. Then, after two or three weeks, you are likely to be fluent in counting to 10 in that language. The same thing goes for our mindsets. If we can devote 10 minutes a day to exercising our value-creating mindset's neural connections, we are going to experience a significant shift in our mindsets in a matter of weeks.

This is now what you need to do. You need to effectively hit the gym for your mind.

A Note About Mindset Exercises

Research has found that there are global exercises that seem to positively influence all of your value-creating mindsets. We discussed most of these in the previous chapter. These exercises include meditation and gratitude journaling.

While these are good exercises to do, if not necessary, I strongly encourage you to identify exercises that are more specifically focused on the value-creating mindset that you want to work on: the growth, open, promotion, or outward mindset.

Mindset researchers have identified six types of activities that are good for activating and strengthening our mindset neural connections. They include watching videos, reading books or articles, listening to podcasts, having discussions with others, journaling, and working on improving your self-talk. Remember that the activities should be focused directly on the value-creating mindset you are working on.

For a whole host of exercises associated with each of the value-creating mindsets, go to this QR code/website.

Constructing a Mindset Development Plan

With this understanding, it is now your job to come up with your "workout" plan. Let me guide you in creating it.

First, write down which value-creating mindset you are going to work on.

Second, journal about why you are focusing on this mindset. Write about how you will be different and better when you adopt it more fully. Also, write about why you feel it is important to develop this mindset.

Doing this journaling effort might sound corny, but it works! Research has repeatedly found that journaling helps us engage with our desires and commitments more deeply.

Third, you need to identify which exercises you want to focus on. Let me give you your base options:

- watching videos
- reading books
- reading articles
- listening to podcasts
- having discussions with others
- journaling
- working on improving your self-talk

To identify which of these exercises will be best for you to focus on, let me have you answer two questions. First, what are the three items in the list that you think will be the easiest for you to do? Second, of those three, which two do you think will have the biggest impact on your mindsets? In other words, from which two do you think you will get the biggest return on your time investment? After answering these two questions, you should have two exercises that you think will be the easiest and most impactful to do. These are the exercises you should start with.

Third, you now need to engage in those activities on a regular basis. My recommendation is at least four days per week and at least 10 minutes per day.

Remember, upgrading your internal operating system is not about a big download, it is about small actions repeatedly taken over time. You have got to put in the work.

In my mind, this isn't too different from gearing up to run a marathon. If we want to run a marathon but have only run a 5k before, the best thing for us to do is to run regularly, and in doing so gradually extend our distance in small increments over time. It takes putting in the reps.

We shouldn't expect any different with our mindsets. If we want more elevated value-creating mindsets, we need to put in the time and effort.

Key Discoveries

Across my experience working with thousands of people on their mindsets, I have learned something that I hope will give you added motivation for consistently hitting the gym for your mindset neural connections.

What I have observed is that over 75 percent of people who create a mindset development plan never actually do the work of engaging with that plan.

This does not mean that their initial awakening efforts have fully gone to waste. But they have stalled out in their journey of becoming transformationally better.

I tell you this not to discourage you, but to encourage you. Look at it this way: If you are one of the few who actually put in the work of elevating your mindsets, you are going to quickly stand apart from your peers in your *becoming better* journey.

But if you are part of the 75 percent that struggles to take the initiative to consistently exercise your value-creating mindset's neural connections, that may be a sign that you need to go deeper with your development, which is where we will go in the next chapter.

Applications for Leadership

It is one thing for a leader to focus on elevating their mindsets. But leaders also need to be aware of and sensitive to the mindsets of those they lead.

In fact, working with organizations and groups on their collective mindsets, I have learned two things. First, if I know the quality of the organization's collective mindsets, I can gain a really clear sense of the quality of its culture. Second, if I can help the organization awaken to and elevate their mindsets, naturally the culture will improve.

I bring this up because I have found that the leaders who vertically develop the most through a focus on mindsets do not work on them in isolation. They work on their mindsets with the people they lead. They are introducing the concept of mindsets to their employees by showing them videos, having them read articles, and discussing these resources in an effort to improve their own and their employees' mindsets. I encourage you to do the same.

19

Deepest-Level Activities to Elevate Your Being Side

No matter who you are, no matter what you did,
no matter where you've come from, you can always change,
become a better version of yourself.

MADONNA

WANT TO INTRODUCE you to someone I have gotten to know through her books who stands out to me as a person with an incredible *becoming better* journey. Her name is Edith Eger, and she is a Holocaust survivor.

If you aren't familiar with her books *The Choice* and *The Gift*, here is a bit of background. Edith Eger grew up as the third daughter in a Jewish family in Hungary. In her early teens, she excelled at gymnastics and ballet and became a member of the Hungarian Olympic gymnastics team. Despite her best attempts to hide her Jewish descent, it was discovered that she was Jewish and she was removed from the gymnastics team in 1942, when she was 15.

Less than two years later, after the German occupation of Hungary, her family was forced to live in a Jewish ghetto before being deported to Auschwitz. Upon arriving, it was Josef Mengele, a physician nicknamed the "Angel of Death" for the deadly experiments he performed on prisoners, who separated her and her sister from her parents. Both of her parents were killed at Auschwitz.

After eight months in Auschwitz, as the Soviets advanced toward the camp, Edith and her sister were part of a group of prisoners who were taken to a series of other camps, including a thread factory in Germany, an ammunition factory near the Czechoslovakia border, and Mauthausen, the camp she called the "place worse than any we [had] yet seen." Surviving a selection line at Mauthausen, she was one of 2,000 prisoners marched to Gunskirchen concentration camp about 34 miles (55 kilometers) away. Only 100 of these prisoners would survive the march.

It was at Gunskirchen, lying in a pile of the dead, in a state where she could not move nor speak, and having a broken back from her abuse, that she was rescued by American soldiers.

At the time she weighed 70 pounds, and it took over six weeks for her to be nursed to the point where she could travel back to her family's home in Hungary. Of the 15,000 Jewish deportees from her hometown, she and her sister were 2 of 70 who survived.

Soon after, at the age of 19, she married another Jewish survivor, Béla Eger, who had fought with the partisans during the war. In 1949, when she was 22, they fled to the United States with their daughter to escape communist threats.

Edith Eger was 90 when she wrote her memoir *The Choice*. Reflecting on her experience arriving in the United States, she shares with her readers:

> I just wanted to be a Yankee doodle dandy. To speak English without an accent. To hide from the past. In my yearning to belong, in my fear of being swallowed up by the past, I worked very hard to keep my pain hidden. I hadn't yet discovered that my silence and

my desire for acceptance, both founded in fear, were ways of running away from myself—that in choosing not to face the past and myself directly, decades after my literal imprisonment had ended, I was still choosing not to be free.

Through my research on trauma, my experience with it, and the fact that over 70 percent of people have experienced it, I have learned that wanting to hide from our past is a common response to our worst experiences. And I found it powerful to learn just how strongly Edith Eger tried to deny her past.

One example of this is when her oldest daughter, a voracious reader at the age of 10, found a book about the Holocaust hidden behind other books on a bookshelf in their home in El Paso. She opened the book to a picture of naked, skeletal corpses piled up in a heap and asked, "What is this?"

For Edith, this was the first time her children's lives were connecting with the past she was adamant to deny. She was caught off guard and immediately became sick. She ran into the bathroom and vomited. From the bathroom, she heard her husband say, "Your mother was there." Edith writes that she had the urge to break the bathroom mirror. *No! No! No!* she wanted to scream. But she stayed frozen in the bathroom, fearing that if she said a word about her past, it would stoke her rage and loss and she would fall into the dark.

Several years later, her daughter was picked up by her date for the high school prom. As her daughter stepped off the porch with her date, Béla called out, "Have a great time, honey. You know, your mother was in Auschwitz when she was your age and her parents were dead." After her daughter left, Edith raged and screamed at her husband, feeling like he spoiled a beautiful evening.

Reflecting on this moment, Edith writes, "Worse than Béla's comment is the fact that I never talked to [our daughter] about it afterward. I pretended not to notice that she was also living two lives—the one she lives for herself and the one she lives for me because I wasn't allowed to live it." She went on to add that at this time in her life, she was "numb, and anxious, isolated, so brittle and sad."

As you can tell, Edith was quite dissociated, unwilling to acknowledge, connect with, and deal with her feelings from the past. This also meant that she was rather unwilling to connect with uncomfortable feelings in the present, which included the fact that she was in denial about how she wasn't very happy, didn't have a sense of self, and wasn't self-directed.

But everything changed for her in the 1960s, when she enrolled in college. At college in her 30s, one of her peer students gave her Viktor Frankl's book *Man's Search for Meaning*. While everything about the book made her uncomfortable, she wound up reading almost all of it in one sitting. This was a turning point for her, and perhaps for the first time she realized that she had been living in survival mode as opposed to living a life of self-direction and meaning.

With greater realization of her unhappiness, and in an attempt to become more self-directed and free, she asked Béla for a divorce.

But her divorce did not bring her the freedom she was hoping for. It didn't liberate her from her anxiety, isolation, brittleness, and sadness. In fact, she writes that her divorce emptied the room of other distractions, of the habitual targets of her blame and resentment, and forced her to sit alone with her difficult feelings. She came to the realization that divorce didn't fix what she thought was broken. And she began to realize that rather than trying to change what was going on outside of her, perhaps she needed to change what was going on inside of her.

Eventually, friends intervened and asked if she'd thought of working through her past.

Her knee-jerk reaction was to think, *Work through the past? I lived it, what other work is there to do?* According to her memoir she simply told her friends, "The past is past," not being ready to even understand this advice. But it was another seed planted on her healing journey.

Over a year after their divorce, Béla took her out for dinner and courageously asked her to get back together. Reflecting on this moment, she writes,

> Now that I have faced myself a little more fully, I can see that the emptiness I felt in our marriage wasn't a sign of something wrong in our relationship, it was the void I carry with me, even now, the void that no man or achievement will ever fill. Nothing will ever make up for the loss of my parents and childhood. And no one else is responsible for my freedom. I am.

Two years after their divorce, they remarried. While she had been successful as a schoolteacher, Edith believed there was more for her in life. She decided she wanted to help people who have gone through trauma and loss as she had. So she went back to school, where she earned an MA in educational psychology in 1974 and a PhD in clinical psychology in 1978. But while she became more open to talking about her past, she had yet to make any efforts to work through it.

Writing about this time, she shares the following in *The Gift*:

> It wasn't until ... I was finishing my training as a clinical psychologist, that I realized the cost of my double life. I was trying to heal others without healing myself. I was an imposter. On the outside, I was a doctor. On the inside, a terrified sixteen-year-old was quaking, cloaked in denial, over-achievement, and perfectionism. Until I could face the truth, I had my secret, and my secret had me.

Edith finished her final clinical internship as a psychologist at William Beaumont Army Medical Center in Fort Bliss, Texas. One day, she arrived at work and was assigned two new patients, both Vietnam veterans, and both paraplegics. She writes, "On my way to see them, I am unaware that one of them will have a life-changing effect on me."

She first met Tom, who was lying on his bed, filled with rage and cursing God and country. In the next room she met Chuck, who was sitting in his wheelchair and shared with Edith how grateful he was to have a second chance at life. This contrast, in and of itself, was a powerful lesson for her. But she writes, "What I still have trouble admitting, however, is that when I first met Tom, his rage thrilled me."

By witnessing Tom's fury, it called out the huge fury in herself. She suddenly had a need to express it and release it. In a later meeting with her therapist, she said she wanted to try expressing her own rage in his presence so he could rein her back in if she were to lose control. She got down on the floor and tried to yell. But she couldn't; she was too scared. Feeling that she needed some weight on her to push against, she told her therapist to sit on her. Almost suffocating, a scream came out of her, "so long and full and anguished that it frighten[ed her]." She couldn't stop screaming. More than 30 years of pent-up anger, hurt, and loss came roaring out of her. It felt so good.

For her, this was a life-changing experience. Why? Because she learned two powerful lessons that countered a belief she had been holding onto her whole life. The first lesson was: feelings, no matter how powerful, aren't fatal. They are temporary. And suppressing feelings only makes it harder to let them go. "Expressing feelings is the opposite of depression," she wrote. The second lesson was: "You can't heal what you can't feel."

From then on, while it was never easy for her to talk about her past, she became willing to do so. She stopped hiding and living in denial.

She realized that her ability to help her patients had to come from a deeper place within her. Her trauma and her healing journey could be a well that she could draw upon, a deep source of understanding that could help her patients heal.

Do you sense a significant shift in her Being Side altitude? She became willing to let go of her Mind 1.0 needs for safety, comfort, and fitting in. She became willing to be unsafe, uncomfortable, and not belong in order to heal, to be herself, and live life in a more self-directed and fulfilling way.

As of this writing, Edith Eger is still alive and in her late 90s. Embracing, working through, and healing from her past allowed her to become a master healer for countless others. She became an internationally renowned psychologist, speaker, and author.

Reflecting on her life in *The Gift*, she writes:

> Surviving Auschwitz was only the first leg of my journey to freedom... As a psychologist; as a mother, grandmother, and great-grandmother; as an observer of my own and others' behavior; and as an Auschwitz survivor, I am here to tell you that the worst prison is not the one the Nazis put me in. The worst prison is the one I built for myself.

Edith Eger's story jars me to my core. I believe there are two reasons why. First, in reading about her awakening to her self-protective prison, I realized more fully the presence of my own self-protective prison that I too wanted to ignore and keep secret. Second, learning about the liberation that can occur by fully acknowledging this prison gave me the permission to seek my own liberation.

It is my hope that you feel similarly.

Through my coaching, I have come to learn that many people live in self-protective prisons that are a product of their past. And their bodies, like Edith's, want to run from their past and their prison. The consequence of this is that they struggle with being mindful, present, introspective, and able to step outside of themselves to observe themselves. But like Edith, what we ultimately need to learn is that it is only by taking the leap of faith to step into the discomfort of the

Becoming the person that
we desire to be and have the
potential to be can't happen
if we are hiding or disowning
parts of ourselves.

_____

past that we are able to heal, rise above it, and more fully become the driver of our lives, instead of the prisoners of self-protection.

Edith writes, "Healing can't happen as long as we're hiding or disowning parts of ourselves. The things we silence or cover up become like hostages in the basement, trying more and more desperately to get our attention."

Putting this quote in the language of this book: *becoming better*, becoming the person that we desire to be and have the potential to be, can't happen if we are hiding or disowning parts of ourselves.

Doing the Deep Being Side Work

As mentioned earlier, our Being Side limitations are not always rooted in past trauma. There could be other things going on, like various forms of neurodivergence, including ADHD.

No matter the cause, the ultimate solution is the same: If we want to *become better*, we need to heal and upgrade our body's internal operating system (i.e., nervous system). We need to break out of our own self-protective prison. Such healing, upgrading, and breaking out will not come about through our typical developmental approach, horizontal development and improving along our Doing Side. It will only come about by engaging in vertical development. Consider Edith Eger's journey. She engaged in horizontal development as she completed her PhD in clinical psychology. But she was still unwilling to fully embrace her past and do the deep work of healing from it. She had to embrace other efforts, which included working with a therapist, going back to Auschwitz, and thousands of little efforts to improve her self-talk. She had to push against her limiting beliefs and exercise more positive mindsets.

When we do this work, we will be able to upgrade from a fearful, self-protective person to a self-directed, inspiring, and value-creating one. To me, Edith Eger is living proof that regardless of our past, we can transformationally *become better*. But that process might entail enlisting the help of professionals.

Neuroscience suggests that if we were to do a brain scan of Edith's brain pre-healing and post-healing, we should expect to find that through her efforts, she improved the collective functionality of her default mode network, salience network, and central executive network. For the rest of this chapter, I will introduce and discuss three deep-level activities that have been found to help people *become better* by upgrading their internal operating systems via improving the collective functionality of these three brain networks. There are likely activities beyond these three that can similarly help, but at the moment, I am not aware of any that have enough research backing to feel comfortable presenting them to you here. I expect that as the field of neuroscience continues to progress, we will be able to add to this list over time.

The three deep-level activities that we'll walk through are psychological therapy, neurofeedback therapy, and psychedelic-assisted therapy. But before we jump into these therapies, let me be clear about something: I am not a trained medical professional. In this chapter, I am simply presenting information that I have learned from reading neuroscientific and psychological research. If you consider engaging in any of these activities, you should first consult with a trusted medical professional.

Now, let's jump in.

Psychological Therapy

There are dozens of psychological therapy approaches designed to help people become better. Covering all such approaches is beyond the scope of this book. But I do want to introduce you to some therapeutic methods that meet two criteria. The first criteria is that the therapeutic approach must have neuroscientific research that supports its effectiveness in improving the functionality of the default mode network, salience network, and/or central executive network. (Let me acknowledge that the number of therapeutic approaches that have been studied by neuroscientists is limited.) The second criteria is that the neuroscientific research on the therapeutic approach needs to have focused specifically on healing from psychological trauma and not other medical conditions like brain injuries, schizophrenia, or Alzheimer's disease.

Using these two criteria as a filter, I have identified three psychological therapy approaches worth bringing to your attention: cognitive behavioral therapy, exposure therapy, and Eye Movement Desensitization and Reprocessing therapy. But before jumping into these three forms of therapy, since throughout this book I have used Brené Brown as an example of someone who has elevated along her Being Side, let me point out that, in her books, she references therapy as being a critical part of her vertical development journey.

Cognitive Behavioral Therapy. Also known as CBT, this is a frontline psychological treatment approach, particularly for post-traumatic stress disorder. It is a form of talk therapy.

CBT is founded on the premise that psychological problems are based, in part, on faulty or unhelpful ways of thinking. As a result, CBT treatment generally involves efforts to *change* one's thinking patterns or cognitions. Generally, this involves interrogating and uprooting negative or irrational beliefs.

A primary emphasis of CBT is on helping individuals to be their own therapists. Thus, CBT involves exercises designed to help one develop better thinking and coping skills in order to rise above problematic emotions and self-sabotaging behaviors.

The American Psychological Association identifies these common CBT exercises:

- learning to recognize one's distortions in thinking that are creating problems, and then reevaluating them in light of reality

- gaining a better understanding of the behaviors and motivation of others

- improving problem-solving skills to better cope with difficult situations

- learning to develop a greater sense of confidence in one's own abilities

- facing one's fears in a structured way

- using role-playing to prepare for potentially problematic interactions with others

- learning how to calm one's mind and relax one's body

CBT has been found to be effective in treating a number of different psychological conditions as effectively as antidepressants, and improving the collective functionality of the brain's three primary processing networks. But while CBT can be effective for some, it is not for all. Research has also revealed that up to one-half of patients do not respond optimally to this form of therapy.

Some of the known disadvantages of CBT include:

- It commonly does not take the past into account. The focus is primarily on "the here and now" and not on resolving and working through past trauma.

- Typically it also does not take one's context or circumstances into account.

- It is generally most helpful for people with mild psychological challenges. It may not be suitable for people with more complex mental health needs.

- It can be difficult and uncomfortable. CBT involves looking at one's anxieties and engaging in work to push back against them.

- Likely because of the point above, CBT has a high dropout rate. It requires significant motivation from the patient.

Exposure Therapy. One specific branch of CBT that has received significant research attention from neuroscientists is exposure therapy. Exposure therapy involves a therapist guiding a patient to imagine reliving their traumatic experience in a safe setting, and doing so in increasingly vivid detail over a number of therapy sessions. Naturally, this process will bring up strong feelings for the patient, but this provides the therapist the opportunity to help the patient work through their feelings. One of the goals of exposure therapy is to help the patient learn that trauma-related memories and cues are not dangerous and do not need to be avoided.

The premise of exposure therapy is that if trauma is avoided and not properly processed, one will develop functional impairment and symptoms of PTSD. So exposure therapy is used to surface the past trauma, help the patient habituate to stimuli that cause distress, reduce anticipatory anxiety, and process the trauma effectively so that they can replace avoidance behaviors with learned adaptive responses. Stated differently, exposure therapy is a process that is designed to take one's trauma out of the driver's seat of their life, allowing the person to take the wheel themselves.

Repeatedly, neuroscience researchers have found that exposure therapy improves the collective functionality of one's salience, default mode, and central executive networks, relieving them of PTSD symptoms; reducing anxiety, avoidance, and reactivity to triggers connected to their past trauma; and widening their window of tolerance.

One of the big challenges associated with exposure therapy is that while it works well for those who engage in it, asking someone to repeatedly relive their trauma, something they might be inclined to avoid, is a formidable request.

Eye Movement Desensitization and Reprocessing Therapy. Also known as EMDR, this is a psychotherapy technique that uses bilateral stimulation, like eye movements, shoulder tapping, or pings in one's ear, as part of the process of working through trauma memories and other distressing life experiences.

EMDR operates on two basic premises. First, it recognizes that past trauma effectively wounds the brain and creates emotional blocks that cause people who have experienced trauma to get stuck in self-protective, self-limiting, and even self-destructive ways of operating. Second, it recognizes that in order for one who has experienced trauma to function at a higher level, they must remove their blocks and heal their wounds. These two premises guide therapists to help their patients step into their past trauma to remove the blocks caused by that trauma and foster the healing that could not occur immediately after one's past traumatic experiences. Doing this deep work allows the patient to rise above their self-protective, self-limiting, and self-destructive ways of operating.

The full name "eye movement desensitization and reprocessing" identifies two objectives of EMDR. The first is to desensitize one's relationship to their past trauma. This involves engaging in bilateral stimulation while a therapist guides one to step back into their traumatic memories. Scientists are not sure why, but the bilateral stimulation reduces the vividness and emotion associated with traumatic memories, which allows one to relive them without being overcome by them. Effectively, this stimulation is a block removal, which opens the door for healing the wounds.

The second objective of EMDR is to reprocess the memories associated with one's past trauma. After having been desensitized to it, the patient is guided by the therapist to change the way their traumatic memories are stored in their brain. This is effectively healing and repairing those wounds.

This entire process allows patients to more fully own and rise above their past. The traumatic experience is still remembered, but the feelings and emotions connected to it are dampened, and the triggers that would previously activate one's fight, flight, or freeze response are diminished. There is an expansion of one's window of tolerance. As with exposure therapy, EMDR allows one to remove their past from the driver's seat of how they process and operate.

Dozens of clinical trials have found that EMDR is one of the fastest and most effective ways for treating post-traumatic stress disorder (PTSD). In one study, researchers found that approximately 85 percent of single-trauma victims with PTSD who participated in three 90-minute EMDR sessions no longer had symptoms of PTSD. And neuroscience research has confirmed that EMDR improves the collective functionality of one's salience, default mode, and central executive networks.

Neurofeedback Therapy

John Mekrut is a neurofeedback expert and the founder of the Balanced Brain Neurofeedback Training Center in North Hollywood, California. When I asked him to describe what neurofeedback therapy is, he simply stated it is "peak performance training for the brain."

This training or therapy primarily leverages the technology of an electroencephalogram, or EEG, which is a non-invasive tool that measures and records electrical brain activity via electrodes placed on the scalp.

Generally, EEGs are used to diagnose, monitor, and, with adaptation, treat brain-related issues. In terms of diagnosis and monitoring, doctors or trained professionals can use an EEG to look at the amount and strength of slow brain waves (delta or theta waves), medium brain waves (alpha waves), and fast brain waves (beta waves) in or between different brain regions. From this information, doctors can diagnose a wide variety of brain-related issues.

For example, doctors have learned that there are electrical patterns in the brain that are unique to ADHD. While EEG is never the sole tool for diagnosing that condition, it is common for people with ADHD to have (1) lower electrical activity in their prefrontal cortex, (2) a higher ratio of slow brain waves to fast brain waves, and/or (3) lower connectivity values in their posterior parietal cortex compared to those without ADHD. These patterns are clear indicators that the connective functionality between the salience, default mode, and central executive networks is weak, resulting in issues related to attention and impulsiveness.

In terms of treatment, EEGs can also be used for a variety of brain-related conditions, including ADHD. Such treatment for ADHD and related issues is called neurofeedback therapy.

Neurofeedback therapy utilizes a technology called brain-computer interfaces, where EEG output can be shown on a screen in the form of a game or a task, providing the patient with real-time feedback about how their brain is functioning. These games and tasks can be set up to help an individual activate certain brain regions and processes, adjust the rhythm or amplitude of various brain frequencies, or inhibit the activation of certain frequencies or regions. Not only does this help the patient gain voluntary control and regulation of their own brain functionality, but it can lead to a strengthening of the connective functionality between brain networks. John Mekrut told me that the power of neurofeedback therapy is that it helps an individual's brain learn what it is like to function more effectively, and it opens up the opportunity to continue doing so outside of a therapy setting.

In the case of ADHD, when patients have fewer fast brain waves or weaker electrical connectivity between brain regions, in a neurofeedback session patients can be incentivized to activate more fast brain waves and increase the connective neural patterns between brain regions. Through this process, patients are able to more properly align their brain's operations, helping them to improve their focus, ability to sustain attention, and overall self-regulation.

Stated simply, neurofeedback therapy is designed to help people train their brain to more readily use healthier patterns.

While neurofeedback therapy is commonly used to treat issues related to ADHD, it is also used in the treatment of anxiety, depression, epilepsy, autism spectrum disorder, insomnia, drug addiction, schizophrenia, sleep disorders, and learning disabilities.

As I discussed in chapter 5, my wife engaged in neurofeedback therapy to help her with her ADHD symptoms, and she has noticed transformational changes in how she operates. It helped her to change or improve many of the traits that she didn't like about herself.

While my wife and others have seen transformational effects, researchers who study the effectiveness of neurofeedback therapy are quick to point out two primary themes. First, we need more research on its effectiveness. Second, existing research indicates mixed effects, meaning sometimes it seems to help and sometimes it does not. But researchers believe that a big reason for these mixed-effect findings is because, historically, most neurofeedback studies have been poorly designed and have not followed the appropriate research standards for neurofeedback treatment. Stated differently, there has been a lot of inconsistency in how researchers have approached neurofeedback therapy in research studies.

Psychedelic-Assisted Therapy

A growing and somewhat controversial body of research that explores the improvement of brain functionality focuses on the use of psychedelics. Psychedelics are a class of psychoactive substances that alter perception, mood, and cognitive processes. When one takes these substances, the effect is generally described as a "trip."

Among the most studied psychedelics are psilocybin, which is found in certain mushrooms; ketamine, an anesthetic with hallucinogenic effects; LSD, also known colloquially as acid or lucy; and MDMA, also known as ecstasy. While these substances are considered "hard drugs," produce hallucinations that can be long-lasting and disturbing, and can lead to increased anxiety, psychedelics are among the safest of the hard drugs if taken in proper dosages. These drugs are not addictive and have an extremely low chance of lethal overdose.

Researchers are finding that if these drugs are used in correct doses and one's "trip" is guided by a trained professional, they can significantly help people who struggle with PTSD, anxiety, depression, addiction, and more. The reasons for this include:

- Psychedelics increase neuroplasticity, which facilitates the rewiring of maladaptive neural circuits and promotes greater cognitive functionality.

- Psychedelics cause an altered state of consciousness that gives people a different perspective on their thoughts, emotions, and behaviors, leading to deeper introspection, insight, and emotional processing than normal.

- Psychedelics can lower individuals' self-protective walls, increasing their ability to introspect and process past trauma.

- Psychedelics can enable increased neuroplasticity and altered states of consciousness, which in turn opens the door for emotional breakthroughs, including acceptance or increases in empathy, that help foster psychological healing.

Altogether, psychedelics can help people experience profound and long-lasting shifts in their perspective, worldview, and sense of self. In fact, research on the treatment of PTSD is finding that psychedelics are among the most effective treatments for addressing PTSD and healing from past trauma.

At a neuroscience level, the reason psychedelics have such a powerful and beneficial effect is because they can, particularly with the help of a professional guide, quickly alter and improve the connective functionality between the three brain regions responsible for how we process our world.

The reality is that it has only been in recent years that the U.S. Food and Drug Administration (FDA) and research review boards have allowed for research on the use of psychedelics for the treatment of psychological disorders. With the little research that has been done, findings have led the FDA to designate psychedelic treatments as "breakthrough therapies," giving them priority status for greater research. So, I suspect that in the near future we will learn a lot more about the role psychedelics can play in our pursuit to *become better* by upgrading our internal operating system.

Key Discoveries

I hope you found Edith Eger's story to be both profound and inspirational. I encourage you to seek out her books. I think that her story helps us connect with some valuable lessons:

1 Because of what we have lived through, our internal operating system can be strongly wired for self-protection, perhaps even to the extent that we ultimately resist *becoming better*.

2 Our wiring for self-protection helps us feel safe, but it ultimately limits us and can cause us to inadvertently hurt others.

3 If we want to become our best selves and someone who creates value for others, we need to do the deep inner work of *becoming better*. And this may involve opening up to our past trauma and seeking healing.

4 It is possible to transformationally *become better*.

Doing the work of upgrading and healing our internal operating system to *become better* might be more difficult for some of us than others, particularly if we have experienced significant past trauma or possess neurodivergence, such as ADHD. So, in addition to doing the *becoming better* strategies covered in the previous two chapters, like reciting self-affirmations to ourselves in the mirror every day or giving dedicatory focus to improving our mindsets, you may need to do some deeper work. In this chapter, I have introduced three possible options to consider, including psychological therapy, neurofeedback therapy, and psychedelic-assisted therapy.

I have seen each of these three forms of therapy, whether for myself or those close to me, help people *become better* in transformational ways. So it is my hope that if you aspire to transformationally *become better*, you might be quicker than Edith Eger to initiate the deep inner work to significantly elevate along your Being Side.

Applications for Leadership

Being a leadership development consultant, I am commonly brought in to work with leaders who are really struggling with their leadership. Many times, I am their last resort. In the coaching process with these struggling leaders, two observations have revealed themselves every time. First, I have discovered that the leader either has significant trauma in their past or they demonstrate strong signals of ADHD, or both. And second, these leaders do not see or believe that there is a connection between their trauma and/or ADHD and how they are showing up as a leader. They are operating in a mental and emotional state similar to Edith's prior to her doing the deep therapeutic work on herself.

Most of the time, I can help these leaders move the needle on *becoming better*. But the reality is that they need more support from trained professionals than I am able to provide if they want to elevate to their full potential within a reasonable time span.

I also observe a lot of good leaders who operate in Mind 2.0, but still trip up at times or are so focused on making short-term progress that they aren't able to operate in a manner that is optimal for long-term value creation. If you happen to be one of these leaders, let me encourage you to consider engaging in the deep-level practices I introduced in this chapter.

You might be like my former self, a person who thought they didn't have trauma in their past but really did, and didn't fully appreciate how this trauma was showing up and impacting almost every interaction they had. Or you might be like my wife, who thought that how she navigated life was normal, but it was actually limited because of her ADHD. Regardless, I hope you create space for simply exploring whether you are being held back by functionality issues associated with your salience, default mode, and central executive networks. Because if you are, you can do something about it. And when you do something about it, you will transformationally *become better*.

Conclusion:
Elevate Along Your Being
Side to Become Better

Life is a lively process of becoming.
DOUGLAS MACARTHUR

IN THE INTRODUCTION to this book, I tried to kindly explain that while I believe we all want to become better, most people do not actually know how to do so.

I proposed the idea that when most people seek to become better, they attempt to walk the development path that they are most familiar with: the *doing better* path. While this is a familiar route, I hope you now fully realize that it is limited in its ability to help us become better. It doesn't get at our internal operating system, and it doesn't improve the neural connectivity of our salience, default mode, and central executive networks.

Thus, I have sought to help you understand that if you really want to become better, you need to consider a different path, one with greater potential for personal transformation: the *being better* path.

This route does not involve a focus on improving our knowledge, skills, and abilities. Instead, it focuses on improving our internal operating system, and ultimately our neurology. Now, this path is not my invention. It is there and it has always been there. I have just tried to shine a light on it in the best ways I know. And, in the process, I've tried to give you the science behind this path.

Throughout this book, I have introduced you to a variety of people. One of the first was Bobby Knight. While he had a brilliant basketball mind, he never seemed to discover the *being better* development path, which ultimately held him back from being his best self. While he accomplished great things in the form of winning national championships, he also possessed an internal operating system that led him to behave in ways that ultimately hurt many of the players he coached. I wish I could go back in time and introduce him to the *being better* path.

Then there are people like Brené Brown and Edith Eger, who for the longest time struggled to become better by treading down the *doing better* development path. But then they stumbled upon and engaged in the *becoming better* path, made significant personal transformations, and then helped shed light on this path so that you and I can more readily walk it ourselves.

These examples help us sense how challenging the *becoming better* development path can be, how powerful it can be, and how transformational it can be.

Let me use Brené Brown's words to describe her *becoming better* journey. In her book *Rising Strong*, Brené writes:

> I don't use the term "revolution" lightly. I've learned a lot about the difference between incremental, evolutionary change and thundering, revolutionary upheaval... What's become clear to me is that the rising strong process can lead to deep, tumultuous, groundbreaking, no-turning-back transformation. The process may be a

series of incremental changes, but when the process becomes a practice—a way of engaging with the world—there's no doubt that it ignites revolutionary change. It changes us and it changes the people around us.

I have also provided you with other examples—like my wife Jena, David Goggins, Max, and even myself—all to help you see that transformationally becoming better is possible.

Not only should you now know it is possible, you should know the three steps for becoming transformationally better:

1   learning what our Being Side is
2   awakening to the quality and sophistication of our Being Side
3   engaging in the work to elevate along our Being Side

Having read this book, hopefully you have clarity on all three of these points. If you do, you now have something that few people have: deep clarity on how to truly and actually *become better*.

Most of all, I hope you realize the most profound message in this book: The process of *becoming better* is fundamentally about healing our minds, bodies, and hearts.

I wish you the best in your journey to do just that. To heal your mind, body, and heart so that you can become more like the ideal version of yourself and have more of the positive impact that you desire to have.

Acknowledgments

A S I REFLECT on the completion of this book, I feel immense gratitude for two groups of people: those who have helped me grow into a better person and those who have helped make this book better. I am deeply thankful to each and every one of you.

To the people who have helped me *become better*, thank you from the bottom of my heart. I wouldn't be the person I am today without you. To the loves of my life—my family, Jena, Hailey, and Spencer—thank you for your unconditional love and unwavering support. To my incredible friends—Gifford, Ben, Brandon, Brian, Scott, Richard, and Kurt—thank you for being people I look up to, for inspiring me to see what's possible, and for loving me along the way.

A special thank-you goes to my therapist, Patricia Torres, for guiding me toward healing my mind, body, and heart.

I am profoundly grateful to one of the best mentors anyone could ask for, Alan Mulally, and his remarkable team member, Sarah McArthur. Your guidance has shaped both my work and my life.

Over the years, I've had the privilege of working with dozens of organizations and thousands of leaders. Across these experiences, I've been blessed to meet, learn from, and collaborate with extraordinary people. Supporting leaders who impact the lives and cultures of others has been one of the greatest honors of my life.

To the countless others who have touched my life—seemingly as angels along my journey—thank you for your grace and presence.

To the people who have helped make this book better, thank you for your passion, commitment, and belief in its potential to touch, transform, and elevate lives. Your contributions have been invaluable in bringing this book to life.

I am especially grateful to the team at Page Two: Trena White; my project managers, Natassja Barry and Beate Schwirtlich; my exceptional content editor, Emily Schultz (whose support I cannot thank enough); my meticulous copy editor, David Marsh; and the talented Page Two team members, including Viktoria Skaper (marketing) and Madelaine Manson (sales). I'm also deeply appreciative of my audiobook partners at Twin Flames Studios.

To the many pre-readers of this book, thank you for your thoughtful feedback, encouragement, and care: Alex Andrews, Selene Antonini, Erin Barnett, William Bland, Lisa Campbell, Tyler Christensen, Alan Diehl, Liz Guthridge, Erik Huso, Pat Louden, Jenny Marshall, Bettina Mihai, Rachel Moser, Mario Patenaude, Kristelle Bach Sim, Chris Spear, Cyndi Wentland, and Kim Ziprik. Your insights have made this book richer and more impactful.

Finally, to you—the reader—thank you. It is my hope that this book serves as a guide and catalyst for your own transformational journey toward *becoming better*.

Notes

Introduction

I have written two previous books: Ryan Gottfredson, *Success Mindsets: Your Keys to Unlocking Greater Success in Your Life, Work, & Leadership* (Morgan James Publishing, 2020); *The Elevated Leader: Level Up Your Leadership Through Vertical Development* (Morgan James Publishing, 2022).

Chapter 1: We Have a Doing Side and a Being Side

a "brilliant, brilliant coach and bigger than life": Jay Bilas, "Jay Bilas: I liked the Bob Knight I knew," ESPN, November 1, 2023, https://www.espn.com/mens-college-basketball/story/_/id/38489269/jay-bilas-liked-bob-knight-knew-died-age-83.

Research on star performers: Herman Aguinis and Ernest O'Boyle, "Star Performers in Twenty-First Century Organizations," *Personnel Psychology* 67, no. 2 (2014), 313–50.

developmental psychologists report that 64 percent of adults: Robert Kegan and Lisa Lahey, *Immunity to Change: How to Overcome It and Unlock the Potential in Yourself and Your Organization* (Harvard Business Review Press, 2009).

few people ever elevate along their Being Side: Andy Andrews, *The Little Things: Why You Really Should Sweat the Small Stuff* (Thomas Nelson, 2017), 148–49.

"When we say success and happiness": Adam Grant, *Hidden Potential: The Science of Achieving Greater Things* (Viking, 2023), ebook, 22.

"Leadership is a matter of 'how to be,' not 'how to do'": Frances Hesselbein, "Frances Hesselbein: How to Be, Not How to Do," interview with the Center for Leadership Studies, July 18, 2019, 9 min., 40 sec., https://youtu.be/Hqouh3jQTE8?si=5Vo8pxgC_YAJPsMe.

only 8 percent of leaders operate in the third stage: PricewaterhouseCoopers, "The hidden talent: Ten ways to identify and retain transformational leaders" (2015), https://osca.co/publications/the-hidden-talent-ten-ways-to-identify-and-retain-transformational-leaders.

Many of these books are like: Stephen R. Covey, *The 7 Habits of Highly Effective People: Powerful Lessons in Personal Change* (Free Press, 2004).

Some of these books are: Brené Brown, *Dare to Lead: Brave Work. Tough Conversations. Whole Hearts.* (Random House, 2018); Simon Sinek, *The Infinite Game* (Portfolio/Penguin, 2019); Adam Grant, *Think Again: The Power of Knowing What You Don't Know* (Viking, 2021).

Chapter 2: What Is Your Being Side?

at least 90 percent of our thinking, feeling, judging, and acting: Timothy D. Wilson, *Strangers to Ourselves: Discovering the Adaptive Unconscious* (Belknap Press, 2004).

living in a state of shame, fear, and disconnection: Brené Brown, *The Gifts of Imperfection: Let Go of Who You Think You're Supposed to Be and Embrace Who You Are* (Hazelden, 2010).

she explores a programming pattern that felt so right: Brené Brown, *Daring Greatly: How the Courage to Be Vulnerable Transforms the Way We Live, Love, Parent, and Lead* (Gotham, 2012).

Chapter 4: Primary Causes of Being Side Differences

at least 75 percent of adults who have ADHD: Edward Hallowell, MD, "The Dangers of Undiagnosed Adult ADHD," ADDitude magazine, March 5, 2024, https://www.additudemag.com/undiagnosed-adult-adhd-diagnosis-symptoms.

people with ADHD fall approximately 30 percent behind non-ADHD people in these abilities: Russell A. Barkley, *12 Principles for Raising a Child with ADHD* (Guilford Publications, 2020).

70 percent of adults have experienced some type of traumatic event: "How to Manage Trauma" infographic, National Council for Mental Wellbeing, 2022, https://www.thenationalcouncil.org/wp-content/uploads/2022/08/Trauma -infographic.pdf.

64 percent of people have experienced toxic situations: Stav Ziv, "We're All More 'Toxic Aware' in 2023," *The Muse*, January 25, 2023, https://www.themuse .com/advice/toxic-aware-introduction-muse-survey.

15 to 20 percent of people are neurodivergent: Nancy Doyle, "Neurodiversity at work: a biopsychosocial model and the impact on working adults," *British Medical Bulletin* 135, no. 1 (2020), 108–25.

Chapter 6: Deepen Your Self-Awareness
the trauma we experience in life: Bessel van der Kolk, *The Body Keeps the Score: Brain, Mind, and Body in the Healing of Trauma* (Viking, 2014).

only 10 to 25 percent of adults with ADHD are actually diagnosed: Steven D. Targum and Lenard A. Adler, "Our Current Understanding of Adult ADHD," *Innovations in Clinical Neuroscience* 11, no. 11-12 (2014), https://www.ncbi .nlm.nih.gov/pmc/articles/PMC4301030.

Chapter 9: Fixed and Growth Mindsets
if you want greater depth on this mindset set: Carol S. Dweck, *Mindset: The New Psychology of Success* (Random House, 2006); Ryan Gottfredson, *Success Mindsets: Your Keys to Unlocking Greater Success in Your Life, Work, & Leadership* (Morgan James Publishing, 2020).

This is demonstrated well in a research study: Carol I. Diener and Carol S. Dweck, "An analysis of learned helplessness: Continuous changes in performance, strategy, and achievement cognitions following failure," *Journal of Personality and Social Psychology* 36, no. 5 (1978), 451–462.

Chapter 12: Inward and Outward Mindsets
I recommend the book *The Art of Possibility*: Rosamund Stone Zander and Benjamin Zander, *The Art of Possibility: Transforming Professional and Personal Life* (Harvard Business Review Press, 2000).

Chapter 14: How Trauma Impacts Our Being Side

This is when I read: Bessel van der Kolk, *The Body Keeps the Score: Brain, Mind, and Body in the Healing of Trauma* (Viking Press, 2014).

studies on adverse childhood experiences (ACEs): For a great book that discusses the research associated with ACEs, see Nadine Burke Harris, *The Deepest Well: Healing the Long-Term Effects of Childhood Adversity* (Houghton Mifflin Harcourt, 2018).

64 percent of people have experienced at least one ACE: U.S. Centers for Disease Control and Prevention, "About Adverse Childhood Experiences," 2024, https://www.cdc.gov/aces/about/index.html.

their life expectancy is 20 years shorter: David W. Brown et al., "Adverse childhood experiences and the risk of premature mortality," *American Journal of Preventive Medicine* 37, no. 5 (2009), 389–96, https://pubmed.ncbi.nlm.nih.gov/19840693.

30 times more likely to commit suicide: S.R. Dube et al., "Childhood Abuse, Household Dysfunction, and the Risk of Attempted Suicide Throughout the Life Span: Findings From the Adverse Childhood Experiences Study," *JAMA (Journal of the American Medical Association)* 286, no. 24 (2001).

7 times more likely to suffer from alcoholism: V.J. Felitti et al., "Relationship of childhood abuse and household dysfunction to many of the leading causes of death in adults. The Adverse Childhood Experiences (ACE) Study," *American Journal of Preventive Medicine* 14, no. 4 (1998), https://pubmed.ncbi.nlm.nih.gov/9635069.

14 times more likely to be a victim of violence: M.A. Bellis et al., "Adverse Childhood Experiences (ACEs) in Wales and their Impact on Health in the Adult Population: Mariana Dyakova," *European Journal of Public Health* 26, no. suppl_1 (2016), https://academic.oup.com/eurpub/article/26/suppl_1/ckw167.009/2448496.

15 times more likely to commit violence: Bellis et al., "Adverse Childhood Experiences."

20 times more likely to be incarcerated: Bellis et al., "Adverse Childhood Experiences."

emotional intelligence is the strongest predictor of performance: Travis Bradberry, "9 Skills You Should Learn That Pay Dividends Forever," 2022, TalentSmartEQ, https://www.talentsmarteq.com/9-skills-you-should-learn-that-pay-dividends-forever.

employees with high emotional intelligence are more likely to stay calm under pressure: Travis Bradberry, "How Emotionally Intelligent People Handle Toxic People," 2022, TalentSmartEQ, https://www.talentsmarteq.com/how -emotionally-intelligent-people-handle-toxic-people.

Daniel Goleman, considered the father of emotional intelligence: Global Leadership Foundation, "Emotional Intelligence," n.d., https:// globalleadershipfoundation.com/deepening-understanding /emotional-intelligence/.

The Hay Group has reported that salespeople: HR.com, "The Importance of Emotional Intelligence in the Workplace: Why It Matters More than Personality," 2005, https://www.hr.com/en/communities/training_and _development/the-importance-of-emotional-intelligence-in-the-wo _eak314gc.html.

What neuroscientists have discovered: Ryan Gottfredson and William Becker, "How past trauma impacts emotional intelligence: Examining the connection," *Frontiers in Psychology*, 14, no. 1067509 (2023).

check out my TEDx Talk: Ryan Gottfredson, "How to Fix Leadership Development," TEDx Talk, Corpus Christi, TX, August 16, 2022, 6 min., 23 sec., https://www.youtube.com/watch?v=Rth6apF1mng.

Chapter 15: How ADHD Impacts Our Being Side

"These three brain networks": Erin Digitale, "Interactions between attention-grabbing brain networks weak in ADHD," Stanford Medicine News Center, December 15, 2015, https://med.stanford.edu/news/all-news/2015/12 /attention-networks-different-in-kids-with-adhd.html.

children with ADHD are four times more likely to develop post-traumatic stress disorder: A.E. Spencer et al., "Examining the association between posttraumatic stress disorder and attention-deficit/hyperactivity disorder," *The Journal of Clinical Psychiatry* 77, no. 1 (2016), 72–83.

10 percent of children have received a formal diagnosis of ADHD: Children and Adults with Attention-Deficit/Hyperactivity Disorder (CHADD), "General Prevalence of ADHD," n.d., https://chadd.org/about-adhd/general-prevalence.

75 percent of adults who have it are undiagnosed: Clinical Partners, "Why is ADHD in women undiagnosed so often?" September 7, 2016, https:// www.clinical-partners.co.uk/insights-and-news/item/adhd-in-women-why-is -it-so-undiagnosed.

Chapter 16: The Differences Between Horizontal and Vertical Development

a necessary condition of elevating along our Being Side: Brené Brown, *Rising Strong: The Reckoning. The Rumble. The Revolution.* (Spiegel & Grau, 2015).

Research on meditation has found: For example, see B. Bremer et al., "Mindfulness meditation increases default mode, salience, and central executive network connectivity," *Nature Portfolio* 12, no. 13219 (2022).

Chapter 17: Starter-Level Activities to Elevate Your Being Side

David shares his transformational journey: David Goggins, *Can't Hurt Me: Master Your Mind and Defy the Odds* (Lioncrest Publishing, 2018).

someone who is still climbing the vertical development mountain: David Goggins, *Never Finished: Unshackle Your Mind and Win the War Within* (Lioncrest Publishing, 2022).

like a bicep curl for our brain: Dan Harris, *10% Happier: How I Tamed the Voice in My Head, Reduced Stress Without Losing My Edge, and Found Self-Help That Actually Works—A True Story* (It Books, 2014).

Research is finding that yoga has the same effects: For more information see R. Ramírez-Barrantes et al., "Default Mode Network, Meditation, and Age-Associated Brain Changes: What Can We Learn from the Impact of Mental Training on Well-Being as a Psychotherapeutic Approach?" *Neural Plasticity* 2019, no. 7067592.

our willingness to engage in prosocial behaviors: For examples see S. Kyeong et al., (2017). "Effects of gratitude meditation on neural network functional connectivity and brain-heart coupling," *Scientific Reports* 7, no. 5058; and G. Tabibnia, "An affective neuroscience model of boosting resilience in adults," *Neuroscience and Biobehavioral Reviews* 2020, no. 115, 321-350.

Habit stacking is taking a current habit: James Clear, *Atomic Habits: An Easy & Proven Way to Build Good Habits & Break Bad Ones* (Avery, 2018).

Chapter 19: Deepest-Level Activities to Elevate Your Being Side

If you aren't familiar with her books: Dr. Edith Eva Eger, *The Choice: Embrace the Possible* (Scribner, 2018); *The Gift: 14 Lessons to Save Your Life* (Scribner, 2020).

It requires significant motivation from the patient: For more information see S. Yuan et al., "Neural Effects of Cognitive Behavioral Therapy in Psychiatric Disorders: A Systematic Review and Activation Likelihood Estimation Meta-Analysis," *Frontiers in Psychology* 2022, no. 853804.

One of the big challenges: For more information see A.P. King et al., "Altered default mode network (DMN) resting state functional connectivity following a mindfulness-based exposure therapy for posttraumatic stress disorder (PTSD) in combat veterans of Afghanistan and Iraq," *Depression and Anxiety* 33, no. 4 (2016), 289–299.

Also known as EMDR, this is a psychotherapy technique: A summary of EMDR effectiveness is provided in Francine Shapiro, "The Role of Eye Movement Desensitization and Reprocessing (EMDR) Therapy in Medicine: Addressing the Psychological and Physical Symptoms Stemming from Adverse Life Experiences," *The Permanente Journal* 18, no. 1 (2014), 71–77.

"peak performance training for the brain": Author interview with John Mekrut, June 2024. The organization's website address is https://thebalancedbrain.com.

the role psychedelics can play: For a helpful source on psychedelic-assisted therapy see K.W. Tupper et al., "Psychedelic medicine: A re-emerging therapeutic paradigm," *Canadian Medical Association Journal* 187, no. 14 (2015), 1054–1059.

Conclusion

I don't use the term "revolution" lightly: Brené Brown, *Rising Strong: The Reckoning. The Rumble. The Revolution.* (Spiegel & Grau, 2015), 253.

About the Author

RYAN GOTTFREDSON, PhD, is a cutting-edge leadership development author, researcher, and consultant. He loves helping organizations vertically develop their leaders, primarily through a focus on mindsets. Ryan is the *Wall Street Journal* and USA *Today* best-selling author of *Success Mindsets: The Key to Unlocking Greater Success in Your Life, Work, & Leadership*; *The Elevated Leader: Level Up Your Leadership Through Vertical Development*; and now, *Becoming Better: The Groundbreaking Science of Personal Transformation*. He is also a leadership professor at the College of Business and Economics at California State University, Fullerton.

Ryan Gottfredson's previous books

Success Mindsets:
Your Keys to Unlocking Greater Success
in Your Life, Work, & Leadership

The Elevated Leader:
Level Up Your Leadership Through Vertical Development

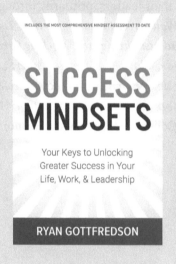

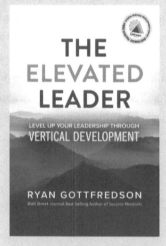

Engaging with Ryan

If you would like additional resources or ongoing support in your *becoming better* efforts, visit Ryan Gottfredson's website at ryangottfredson.com. On this website, you will find

- Communities of Practice to join

- a newsletter to subscribe to

- personal assessments

- access to a wide variety of resources, including books, articles, and videos, all designed to help you walk up the *becoming better* development path.

Ryan also works with organizations, groups, teams, and people to help them *become better*. If you would like him to help you, your organization, your group, your team, or your leaders transformationally *become better*, you can contact him at ryangottfredson.com/contact.

And, of course, Ryan would love to connect with you on all social media platforms.

- 🅵 RyanGottfredsonPhD
- 🅸🅽 linkedin.com/in/ryangottfredson
- ▶️ @RyanGottfredsonPhd
- 𝕏 @RyanGottfredson
- 📷 @ryangottfredson

Made in United States
Troutdale, OR
06/03/2025

31866419R10184